U-Boat: the secret menace

U-Boat

David Mason

the secret menace

Pan/Ballantine

Editor-in-Chief: Barrie Pitt
Art Director: Peter Dunbar

Military Consultant: Sir Basil Liddell Hart
Picture Editor: Robert Hunt

Design Assistants: Gibson/Marsh
Cover: Denis Piper
Research Assistant: Yvonne Marsh
Cartographer: Richard Natkiel
Special Drawings: John Batchelor

Photographs for this book were especially selected from the following Archives: from left to right page 9 Bibliothek fur Zeitgeschichte; 12 Suddeutscher Verlag; 20 Ullstein; 21 Ullstein; 22 Sado Opera Mundi/Popperfoto; 28 Popperfoto; 29 Imperial War Museum; 31 Ullstein; 32-33 Ullstein; 33 Sudd. Verlag; 34 IWM; 35 Sudd. Verlag; 38-39 Sado Opera Mundi; 41 Imperial War Museum; 42 Sado Opera Mundi/US Navy; 43 Sudd. Verlag/Sado Opera Mundi; 47 IWM; 48 Sado Opera Mundi/IWM; 50 Bibliothek fur Zeitgeschichte; 52-53 Sudd. Verlag; 55 Sudd. Verlag; 56-57 IWM; 58 Bibliothek fur Zeitgeschichte; 59 Sudd. Verlag; 62 IWM; 65 Sudd. Verlag/Bibliothek fur Zeitgeschichte; 66-67 Ullstein; 69 Sado Opera Mundi; 74-75 Ullstein; 85 IWM; 88-89 IWM; 91 Sudd. Verlag; 92-93 Sudd. Verlag; 94-95 Sado Opera Mundi; 101 Bibliothek fur Zeitgeschichte; 102-103 Sado Opera Mundi; 106-107 Keystone; 110-111 IWM; 114-115 US Navy; 116-117 US Navy; 118 IWM; 119 Ullstein; 121 Ullstein; 124-125 Bibliothek fur Zeitgeschichte; 128 US Navy/Sudd. Verlag; 129 Sudd. Verlag; 130-131 IWM; 132-133 IWM; 134-135 Keystone; 136 Bibliothek fur Zeitgeschichte; 141 US Navy; 145 Keystone; 146-147 Ullstein; 158-159 Keystone; 159 IWM; 160 Bibliothek fur Zeitgeschichte.

The author is grateful to Houghton Mifflin Company, Boston, and Cassell & Co. Ltd., London, for permission to quote from Winston S. Churchill's 'The Second World War' on pages 13 and 153, and to Athenaum Verlag, Frankfurt, for permission to quote from Admiral Karl Doenitz s 'Ten Years and Twenty Days' on pages 68, 86, 87, 138 and 143.

Contents

The undersea war

Introduction by Barrie Pitt

On the wall of an office in Admiralty Arch in London, there was displayed for many years a chart entitled 'Chronological Diagram of Principal Events, 1939–1945' The second line of this impressive document shows in blue and red columns, side by side, the quarterly losses of Allied shipping in thousands of tons (blue) and the losses of German U-Boats (red). During the first half of the war, the blue columns reach further and further upwards with heart-breaking and tragic regularity, while alongside them the stubby little red columns seem to limp insignificantly towards disaster.

Then suddenly, between March and June 1943, an extraordinary change takes place. From one quarter to the next, a complete reversal occurs and from then on the tall red columns march triumphantly to the end of the chart, while the blue columns sink lower and lower and finally disappear altogether. As a graphic synopsis of the Battle of the Atlantic, this line on that chart could hardly be improved upon, and as a diagram of the peril through which Britain and the whole of the free world passed, it is a revelation.

In this book, David Mason has clothed in lucidly-written prose the stark skeleton of that chart. From the moment in 1935 when the then Captain Karl Doenitz was summoned by his superior, Admiral Erich Raeder to take over the reformation of Germany's U-Boat arm, until the final bitter endings among the chaos and wreckage of the U-Boat pens in harbours from Schleswig-Holstein to Bordeaux, the intricate, fascinating story is clearly and excitingly traced.

And what a story it is!

Despite the flood of film and fiction from British and American sources since 1945 portraying our merchant-seamen as gallant rough diamonds and their enemies, the U-Boat crews, as evil, cold-hearted criminals, even the most impressionable amongst us have always known in our heart of hearts that all submarines, whether 'ours' or 'theirs', are crewed by brave men with enormously high morale and a technical command of specialist skills which compels admiration.

This was as true of the U-Boat arm then, as it is today of the Americans and Britons crewing the Polaris submarines – as readers of this fine account will learn. Even at the end, with their radius of action hopelessly cramped by lack of fuel and their Fatherland in ruins, the U-Boat crews ached for action; and by 1945, techniques of under-water warfare had advanced far beyond those used in the first winter of the war, when Lieutenant Gunther Prien had taken his tiny U-47 into Scapa Flow and sunk the *Royal Oak*.

By now the skills necessary for commanding and using the U-Boat were reaching up towards today's qualifications, when the knowledge and expertise of a professional scientist or engineer are essential behind the periscope; and it is a virtue of David Mason's book that as much of this kind of knowledge as is necessary for the reader to understand is included within the text.

The U-Boat war was a vitally important aspect of the gigantic conflict known as World War II, for it came closer to gaining victory for Hitler than almost any other weapon in his vast armoury. This book does full justice to its subject, and to the men who fought beneath the waves.

The fleet is built

Early on the morning of October 4th 1918, a U-Boat in the Mediterranean, in the middle of an attack on a heavily protected merchant convoy, went out of control, turned on its head, and began a plummeting dive to the bottom. It sank to the danger level of 200 feet, then past it to 300 feet, and under the immense and increasing pressure two of the reserve air tanks burst. To save his crew from a needless extermination the commander dropped all thoughts of evading the enemy, ordered all the remaining air tanks to be blown, and threw the engines full astern to correct the downward dive.

The U-Boat immediately reversed its course, and with the tanks full of compressed air shot up through the depths like a champagne cork and crashed to the surface, under the very noses of a British cruiser and its accompanying destroyers. Hit by their barrage of shellfire, the boat began to take in water, but with the supply of compressed air exhausted, another dive was out of the question, and the commander had no alternative but to abandon ship. The chief engineer and six other hands went down in the process of scuttling the boat, while the remainder of the crew were rescued by a destroyer and taken to Malta.

It was the beginning, for the commander, of many months of confinement in British prison camps, during which time he had ample opportunity to ponder the future of the U-Boat in warfare. Such thinking as he did was put to excellent use. On his release, assured by his superiors that the U-Boat would once again become part of the German Navy, he rejoined the service, and although that assurance was not immediately fulfilled he rose steadily through the ranks during the next seventeen years to command the battle cruiser *Emden*. Then in the summer of 1935 Grand Admiral Raeder relieved him of that command and charged him instead with a task which at first he considered something of a consolation prize, but which turned out to represent the culmination of his life's ambition – that of commanding the new U-Boat arm of the rebuilt German Navy.

That officer's name was Karl Doenitz.

In intervening years Doenitz had completely forgotten his old love for the U-Boat. Under the terms of the treaty of Versailles, Germany was prevented from building them, and Doenitz had entirely settled to his life as a surface sailor. But on March 16th 1935 the Treaty of Versailles was repudiated, and a month later was superseded by the Anglo-German Naval Agreement. Under its terms Germany volunteered to restrict the strength of its Navy to 35 per cent of that of the British Navy, except that the U-Boat arm would be

Architect of the U-Boat campaign, Admiral Karl Doenitz

9

allowed to build up to 45 per cent of British submarine capacity, and even, in special circumstances and after giving due notice, up to 100 per cent, with corresponding restrictions in the strength of other departments.

The agreement on the potential size of the U-Boat arm was based on no altruistic motive by the British, and involved no great sacrifice on their part. They themselves saw little future for the submarine in the navies of the world, particularly their own. The principal task of the British navy, evolved during centuries of tradition, was the protection of Britain's trade routes, and future strategy was based on that concept. It was, however, a defensive role for which the submarine, essentially an offensive strike weapon, was fundamentally unsuited. Consequently the British kept down the numbers of their submarines, and even by 1939 had massed a fleet of only 57.

Signatures were put to the Anglo-German Naval agreement on June 18th, and ten days later a ceremony took place in the shipyard at Kiel which showed that the years since the First World War had not been wasted by German engineers. It was the commissioning of U-1. In those critical years, the nucleus of the future U-Boat arm had been painstakingly and surreptitiously built up. Two U-Boats, for example, had been built for the Finnish and Turkish Navies, but handed over only after extensive 'testing' by a variety of young men who officially belonged to the 'Anti-Submarine School'. After this secret training, these young men became the backbone of the newly permitted U-Boat arm. During 1934, a number of heavily guarded sheds were constructed in the shipyards at Kiel, and it was from one of these, in June of the following year, that the first of the new U-Boats emerged. Others followed in quick succession, and by the end of September there was a flotilla of nine.

Doenitz, with a clean sheet on which to start, attacked his new task with relish and enthusiasm. No German submarine had existed during the preceding fifteen years, and all the young men who had taken part in the secret training were children when the First World War ended. With Doenitz now, only a handful of submariners had stayed in the navy from that war to become members of the new U-Boat arm, notably* Captain Thedsen, who now held the position of Flotilla Engineer. Doenitz was therefore in a position to mould his crews and his tactics along the lines he wanted, for out of the limited experience of operations in the First World War no specific guide lines had emerged which the newly constituted U-Boat arm could follow, no 'instruction manual' had been compiled for Doenitz and his men to read and obey. He was free to work out and exploit his own theories, and in his own mind he was

clear about the principles on which they were based.

He reckoned, for example, that the U-Boats would have minimal effect unless they were able to operate in groups. That was one of the main lessons which Doenitz had gleaned from his experience at the end of the First World War. Then, when the German U-Boat effort was at its height, in three months of the spring of 1917 no less than 800 ships had been sunk, totalling nearly two million tons. Faced with these disastrous figures, the British prime minister, Lloyd George, had forced the Admiralty's hand and compelled the introduction of the convoy system, to replace the then current policy of allowing merchant ships to sail independently. That move, Doenitz recalled, together with the total failure of the U-Boats in the matter of communication and co-operation, had brought an immediate and drastic reduction in the number of vessels sunk. Should the enemy again resort to the convoy system, Doenitz planned, as the best possible method of operation, to form packs of U-Boats into a wide concave curve into which the enemy would penetrate. The first U-Boat to make a sighting would then fall back, keep contact, and communicate the position of the enemy to the others in the formation, who would close on the ships from the flanks and from behind like the jaws of a gigantic trap. As his training programme got under way Doenitz organised, in 1937 and 1939, extensive 'war games' in the North Sea, in which his conception of U-Boat tactics was thoroughly vindicated.

Doenitz also thought a great deal about the size of submarine vessel he wanted, and examined the problem in the light of his own notion of the role of the U-Boat in future warfare, as a unit in a 'killer pack' operating against merchant ships sailing in convoy under escort. Admittedly, a large U-Boat had the advantage in speed, greater torpedo carrying capacity, heavier armaments for self-defence, wider range, and better crew comfort. In favour of small submarines, on the other hand, Doenitz noted their greater manoeuvrability, their ability to dive quickly in an emergency, and their better surface concealment. In addition, he had to consider the terms of the Anglo-German Naval Agreement, which restricted the total permitted tonnage of the U-Boat arm, but placed no limit on their numbers. Doenitz maintained that four small U-Boats were a far more powerful force than a single one four times larger, since together they could cover a greater area of the ocean, and enjoyed far better prospects of encountering the enemy. Having regard to all the relevant factors,

The 'Weddigen' flotilla; early type II U-Boats — 'Dugouts' — commissioned before 1940

On the bridge, officers and hands relax after a successful trip

Arming the U-Boats, the stern torpedoes are loaded

Doenitz concluded that the optimum size for the majority of his fleet was about 500 tons, and this opinion was confirmed, in extensive tests by the performance of his Type VII U-Boat.

This design, of which Doenitz had ten by late 1935 in a flotilla of twenty-four, had four torpedo tubes in the bows and one in the stern, and carried twelve to fourteen torpedoes. It handled well under water, could make 16 knots on the surface, and could be totally submerged within 20 seconds of the order to dive being given. Minor modifications initiated by Chief Engineer Thedsen increased its original size to 517 tons and boosted its somewhat limited fuel capacity, so that its range was extended from a restricted 6,200 miles to a respectable 8,700 miles.

In all this advanced reasoning, however, Doenitz had reckoned without Naval High Command, who, having none of his insight into how group tactics were shaping up in practice, continued to visualise for the U-Boats the same role which they had occupied at the end of the First World War – that of solitary raiders operating independently for extended periods far from base. Almost all U-Boats, they insisted, should be heavily armed on deck to be capable of engaging the enemy in a surface gun battle with confidence, should have great torpedo-carrying capacity, and should have an extremely wide radius of action. Naval High Command therefore opted for the bigger U-Boat, and despite Doenitz's protests, gave priority to the building of 'U-Cruisers' of 2,000 tons.

It was the first of many disagreements which Doenitz and his High Command were to suffer in the course of the coming years. A further dispute arose immediately over the numbers of U-Boats necessary for the conduct of a future war, and over their priority in the broad scheme of naval construction. As the training period wore on, Doenitz grew more and more firm in his conviction that an early war was likely, and that Britain was certain to be on the side of the enemy. He therefore asked for a fleet of at least 300 U-Boats, which he deemed would be effective in their role against the convoys as he visualised it. The German naval building programme was drawn up in the 'Z-plan' which envisaged the construction of six battleships, eight cruisers, four aircraft carriers, several light cruisers, and 233 U-Boats – but not until a planned completion date in 1948!

Given his 300 U-Boats, built at a fast rate, Doenitz maintained that he could strike an early and decisive blow at the enemy. At any time he could have 100 boats actually operating against the convoys, 100 on the way to and from the area of operations, and 100 re-equipping in German ports. With a force of 100 U-Boats permanently in the front line, Germany would be able to cripple the trade routes of the greatest maritime power in the world, routes which had long been vital to the life of the British nation. Along them, in a constant stream of cargo ships, had to be brought not only a considerable proportion of the food for the densely populated island, but also nearly all the supplies of ore and fuel, as well as vehicles and weapons, which Britain would find vital for the prosecution of a major war.

That her trade routes were the one vulnerable spot by which Britain's economy could be folded, her morale crumpled, and her people and government brought to their knees, was in no doubt in Doenitz's mind. But the view that the U-Boat was the one weapon which could play the critical role in isolating the country from its outside resources was shared by few among Doenitz's superior officers – by few, indeed, of his contemporaries on either side, save of course Winston Churchill.

Churchill was later to write: 'The only thing that ever really frightened me during the war was the U-Boat peril. . . . our lifeline, even across the broad oceans, and especially in the entrances to the Island, was endangered. I was even more anxious about this battle than I had been about the glorious air fight called the Battle of Britain.' He subsequently added: 'The U-Boat attack was our worst evil. It would have been wise for the Germans to stake all upon it.'

Doenitz wanted to stake all upon it. He had demanded his 300 U-Boats. He had received, by the time war broke out, fifty-six.

13

The weapon and the foe

Before the Second World War, and during its early years, until events imposed a different complexion on its role, the U-Boat was primarily a surface vessel. Doenitz himself, pointing out the fundamental misconception of the layman who thought of the U-Boat as working perpetually submerged, described it as a 'diving-vessel', designed to travel for most of the time on the surface, and plunge under water only to escape an attacking destroyer or aircraft, or to carry out a torpedo attack in daylight.

The U-Boat had two separate means of propulsion. Two powerful diesel engines drove it forward at speed on the surface, but as soon as it submerged they had to be turned off. They needed oxygen, and when the air intakes fell below the surface, their only source was the supply of oxygen inside the U-Boat itself. The powerful diesel engines would consume that in an instant, and the U-Boat would splutter to a halt with an asphyxiated crew. Instead, at the moment she submerged, the engineers switched over to two battery-driven electric motors. The batteries weighed several tons, and could propel the boats, the early designs at least, at a maximum speed of about eight knots. At more economical speeds, the battery would keep the U-Boat moving for about twenty-four hours, and could take her about 60 miles submerged. After that, the batteries ran flat and it was essential to return to the surface, where the diesel engines came into use again, not to drive the boat, but to work as generators and recharge the batteries – a two to three hour task if the full supply of energy had to be restored.

The main core of the U-Boat's construction was the pressure hull, a long steel cylinder divided into compartments by bulkheads. For the comfort, health, and efficiency of the crew, the interior pressure was maintained at approximately the same level as the outside atmosphere. As the boat submerged, however, the external pressure increased rapidly and severely limited the depths to which a commander dared to take his craft. Under extreme pressures, sixteen tons per square foot at 500 feet for example, the plates began to crack, water seeped in, and it was not long before the vessel sank to the bottom of the sea.

Attached to the outside of the pressure hull were the ballast tanks, equipped with a water valve below and an air valve on top. When filled with air, they lent the boat sufficient buoyancy to keep the heavy pressure hull, packed tight with its complex steel equipment, afloat with the conning tower and decks clear of the water. When both the water valves and the air valves were opened, sea water forced its way into the tanks, expelled the air, and reduced the total buoyancy of the boat, so

14

that it began to sink. The boat could then be controlled in its upward and downward motion, and could be brought back to the surface, either by pumping out the sea water mechanically, or by closing the air valve in the ballast tanks, and blowing in compressed air to force out the sea water through the water valve. Adjustments in depth and trim could also be made after the fashion of an aircraft, by driving the boat through the water and adjusting the bow and stern diving rudders to propel the boat upwards and downwards against the resistance of the water.

The ballast tanks, carried on the outside of the boat, could be less sturdily constructed than the pressure hull, since while the boat was submerged they contained sea water, and were not therefore subjected to the vastly unequal pressure which constituted the grave danger to the main hull at great depths. For the same reason the fuel tanks, also carried outside the pressure hull, were of unusual construction. They were open to the sea water underneath, and the fuel intake valve to the diesel engines was placed at the top of the tank. As the fuel was used up, sea water was admitted underneath it to keep the tanks full, and since the less dense fuel oil floated on top of the water, no salt water was admitted into the engine. With this system, the expenditure of fuel oil left no air space in the tank, either to provide unwelcome buoyancy when the U-Boat was required to submerge, or to cause the tanks to crumple like burst paper bags when the submarine went deep.

The U-Boat's strike power lay principally in its torpedoes – self-propelled containers of high explosives which were themselves like miniature U-Boats, and which went through several stages of development. At first they were driven by compressed air, which left a conspicuous wake of white bubbles behind the torpedo and gave the enemy ample time to take avoiding action. Later models incorporated an electric motor driven by a storage battery, which made them almost invisible. Their method of ignition also developed in the light of experience. Early torpedoes were percussion ignited, and would explode only on contact with the ship. Many of them proved faulty, however, either failing to ignite on contact, or failing to run at precisely the depth set for them, and passing harmlessly below the ship to run on until their motors expired. With the magnetic ignition incorporated in later models, they were designed to explode when entering the magnetic field set up by a ship at sea, and the depth setting therefore became less critical. Even if they exploded below a ship's hull, the strong shock waves under water almost invariably resulted in the vessel's back being broken.

Torpedoes had in their noses an 'arming device', in the form of a small propeller. While in storage, or being carried in the ship, the torpedo's detonating cap was positioned safely clear of the hammer which fired it. Only after the torpedo had left the U-Boat and was on its way to the target did this propeller, revolved by the action of the torpedo driving through the water, turn a screw which moved the hammer and detonator into line.

For the men who crewed the submarine and fired these torpedoes, life in the service was unique, both in its difficulties and in its appeal. A full complement – forty-four officers and men in the case of a Type VIIC U-Boat – lived together at sea in cramped conditions for weeks on end. As they set off for a patrol, every available cubic metre of space was packed with food for the journey. Fresh food was stacked where it was most accessible, often in the crew's normal living compartments. When it had gone, the cooks started on the tinned and dried food, and since that had to be eaten in precisely the reverse order that it had been stored, the health and morale of the men depended to some extent on the intelligence and foresight with which the food had been packed. This was just one small example of the kind of far-sighted planning which had to go into the preparations for a patrol in the U-Boat service.

Exercise was of course virtually impossible. There was no prospect of taking a walk, no space even for more than a limited repertoire of 'physical jerks'. On patrol, even when off duty, a man's share of fresh air was confined to his turn on the small deck. And this, inevitably, was brief. Access from the U-Boat's deck to its interior was through a hatch large enough to admit only one man at a time and since the boat could not dive until everybody was below, a crash dive was impossible if a queue of men was waiting at the hatch. The number of men on deck was clearly limited to a handful, and it was a long time before each sailor's turn came round again.

And there was the tension, the waiting during an action to see whether the destroyers that escorted an enemy convoy would find the U-Boat and attack. One terrible noise told a crew that their U-Boat had been located – the 'ping' against the hull from the Allies' earliest anti-submarine device, the 'asdic'. Named after the initials of the Allied Submarine Detection Investigation Committee, which developed it in 1917, this device was well known to the Germans from extensive publicity between the wars. The asdic consisted of a transmitter-receiver encased in a dome on the bottom of a destroyer. At its heart was a quartz crystal which, when an alternating electric current was applied, oscillated and sent out sound waves through the water. When the waves struck an object they were reflected and picked up again by the

How the submarine works

1

2

To dive a submarine in the quickest possible time the main ballast tanks along the sides were opened to release the air in them. These then flooded with sea water. At the same time the hydroplanes were set to the angle shown in Fig I, and fastest possible forward speed was attained to make them have effect. If the stern hydroplanes were reversed too near the surface the submarine would dive steeper but the propellers would come out of the water stopping the craft. Once below the surface this could be done to make a steep dive. Trim tanks forward could also be flooded to put the bow down. Once down to depth the trim tank water was pumped to the aft tank and hydroplanes set to Fig II to level off. To surface, compressed air was blown into the main ballast tanks to make the craft lighter. Too much at once would make her pop like a cork to the surface and only in an emergency was this done. Fig III shows hydroplane position for normal surfacing.

3

Type IIA

Based on the UB II series of WW I boats the II A was mainly used for training purposes. When on actual operations the AA armament was increased to 2 × 20 mm guns.

Displacement
254/303 tons
Dimensions
$134\frac{1}{4} \times 13\frac{1}{2} \times 12\frac{1}{2}$ feet
Machinery
2-shaft diesel/electric motors, BHP/SHP 700/360 = 13/7 knots
Bunkers and radius
OF 12 tons; 1,050/35 at 12/4 knots
Armament
One 20 mm AA gun; three 21-inch torpedo tubes (all foward – six torpedoes or eight mines)
Complement
25

Asdic

This valuable aid to 'U' boat destruction used a system similar to that used by a bat to navigate. A signal was transmitted from the ship. If this signal struck an object under water, it bounced back to a receiver. The time it took to get back was calculated to give the range of the object. The longer the interval, the longer the range. The 'cone' of the signal could be swung through 360° and the Asdic operator would spend hours 'sweeping' right round the ship. The dotted cone gave a wide search area and once a 'U' boat was located the two narrow cones enabled a much more accurate 'fix' to be given to the bridge for action. Fish shoals, changes of water temperature and disturbance put Asdic on many a false scent but without it the 'U' boat war would have had a very different climax.

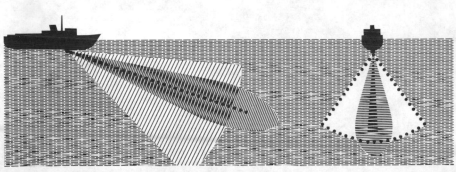

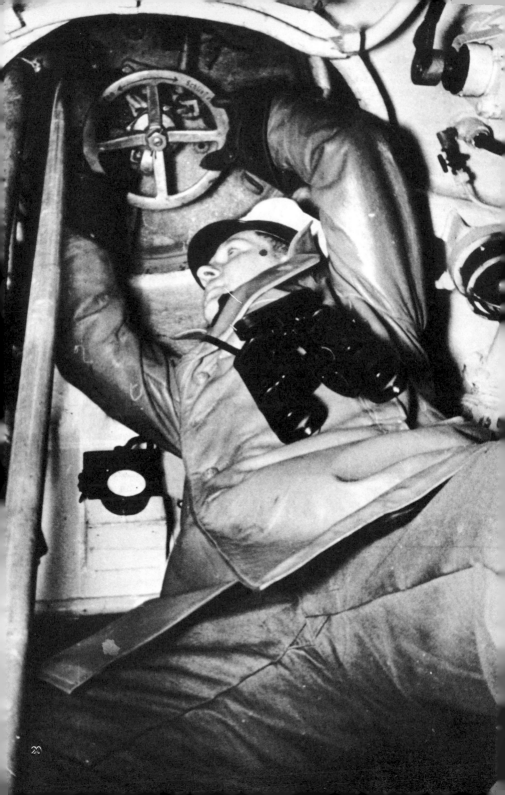

20

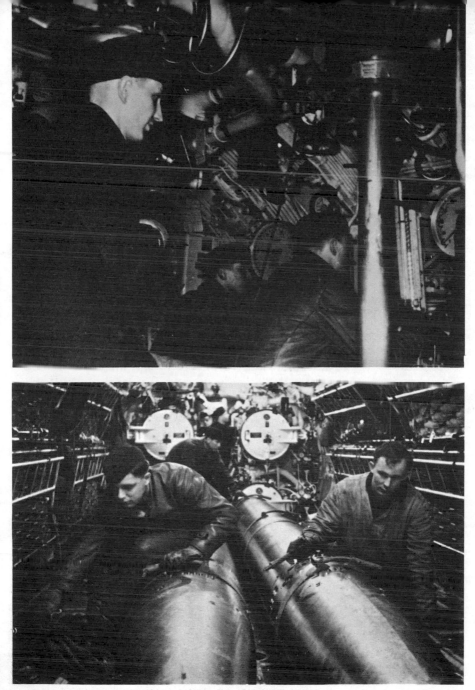

Left Ready to dive, the commander, last man to go below, clamps down the hatch. *Top* The officer in charge of depth control equipment and his hands keep a keen eye on their gauges. *Bottom* Dangerous and dirty, the men who handled the torpedoes had one of the toughest jobs

21

Above Conning tower watch; the officer needed protection against Atlantic spray and winds. *Right* Periscope watch; navigation under sea presented tricky problems

receiver, and the operator knew he had made a contact. By moving slowly, and plotting the bearings of the echoed 'ping', an operator could pin point the direction and range of the object, and the destroyer could attack. Two drawbacks gave the U-Boats their chance of escape. In the first place contact could only be held by means of the asdic up to a certain distance from the U-Boat. When a destroyer came sufficiently close to drop its depth charges, the 'ping' was lost and the destroyer's crew could only guess at the exact position of the U-Boat, which meant that if it moved fast enough it could often evade the main weight of an attack, and escape with only superficial damage. Secondly, the early asdic gave no indication of the depth of the obstacle, and it too could only be estimated.

For the men in the U-Boat, the consequence of their own attack was all too often a fearsome duet played out by the destroyer's engines and its asdic, first the noise of the engine as it bore down on them, then the 'ping' of the asdic as it picked up a contact, then again the engines as it moved on to take another more precise sounding. And finally there was the explosion. If the depth charging was accurate the tremendous force of the explosives, accentuated by the concentration of shock waves under water,

would send the boat pitching and yawing as if in a storm. Then the U-Boat was almost certainly on the way to the bottom. On rare occasions, it was possible to surface and escape before the boat sank, but generally there was little chance of diving overboard and swimming to a raft, little prospect of being picked up by the enemy and taken to a prison camp on land to sit it out until the end of the war. There was just the water pouring in, and the submarine being crushed as it sank to depths its pressure hull could never withstand, or lay on the bottom, until the oxygen was used up.

Yet there was never any shortage of volunteers for the service. The job, the companionship, the sense of working as a small team, these kept the men coming into the U-Boat arm, and kept morale high right to the end.

Problems of war: September 1939 to May 1940

When, on September 3rd 1939, Britain declared war on Germany, forty-six of Doenitz's fifty-six U-Boats were ready for action, but only twenty-two were suitable for operations in the Atlantic. The other twenty-four were small U-Boats, Type II of 250 tons displacement, and their operational range made them suitable only for action in the North Sea.

They were meagre forces with which to go to work, for even of the twenty-two, a maximum of only seven could be actively engaged at any one time in operations against shipping in the Atlantic. Far from disrupting enemy communications and bringing the British to early terms, Doenitz knew that they could do no more than inflict a few odd pin pricks.

The effectiveness of these pin pricks was, moreover, further reduced by the rules within which the U-Boats were allowed to operate. Strict conditions laid down in the *Prize Ordinance* stipulated that a U-Boat must first surface before it could halt and examine a merchant ship. If it were then entitled to sink the ship, because for example it was carrying contraband cargo for the enemy, the U-Boat first had to ensure the safety of the ship's crew by taking them on board – a palpable impossibility in the case of an already crowded submarine. Only if a U-Boat encountered merchant ships sailing under escort, or merchant ships which resisted when called upon to halt or troop transports, was it permitted to take action without the prior need of inspection. This obligation to arrest and inspect of course opened the U-Boat to attack from any vessel which was in fact armed. Being only lightly armed above decks themselves, the small and medium sized U-Boats were extremely vulnerable.

A further complication arose on the outbreak of hostilities when France declared herself at war with Germany. Hitler, anxious to avoid an open clash with France despite the nominal declaration of war, immediately issued an order to U-Boats forbidding any action against French ships except in defence.

The situation was still further confused by the circumstances surrounding the firing of the first torpedo 'in anger'. On the day war was declared Lt Cdr Lemp in command of U-30, sighted a passenger liner which he claimed was off the normal shipping routes, had no lights on, and was steering a zig-zag course. Lemp came to the conclusion that the vessel was a troopship. He established its identity as British, and acted immediately on his entitlement to attack it. His torpedoes struck home, and the ship sank with the loss of 128 lives. Unfortunately the ship proved to be not a troopship at all, but the passenger liner *Athenia* sailing from Britain to the United States, and most of U-30's victims were civilians.

23

Left The passenger liner 'Athenia', sunk by Lt. Lemp on the first day of war. *Below* U-30, the boat which did the job, with others from the 'Salzwedel' flotilla at Hamburg before the war. *Bottom* shocked and weeping, survivors from the 'Athenia' are taken on board a Norwegian tanker

The British government immediately accused the Germans of waging unrestricted warfare in contravention of international law, The German government, on the other hand, denied the charge, and as Lemp made no mention of the action in his wireless reports, it was not until the end of September, when U-30 docked and Lemp was able to report personally to Doenitz, that the truth of the affair came to light. Lemp's action, however much it had been in good faith, was in direct contravention of Hitler's strict instruction to wage war in accordance with the prize regulations, and the German government continued to maintain that no U-Boat had been responsible for the *Athenia's* sinking. Naval High Command was instructed to keep the matter secret, and Kommodore Doenitz was obliged to order Lemp to expunge the record from his war diary, and replace it with a page omitting reference to the incident.

In a further attempt to discount the involvement of a U-Boat in the tragedy, the German Propaganda Ministry, which would have done better to let the matter rest, broadcast the assertion, which gained scant credence anywhere, that the *Athenia* had in fact been sabotaged on the instructions of Winston Churchill, then First Lord of the Admiralty, in order to discredit the German nation as having first broken the rules of sea warfare.

The immediate effect of the *Athenia's* loss was to cause Hitler, still anxious to avoid open hostilities with Britain and France, to issue another strict order confining the activities of the U-Boats, by instructing them in future not to sink any passenger ships, of any nation, whether in enemy service or not, and whether or not they were sailing in convoy.

To Naval High Command, it appeared that the Government was imposing impossible restrictions on the activities of its already inadequate resources, but gradually, by stages, those limitations on U-Boat activity were relaxed. On September 23rd Hitler, at Admiral Raeder's insistence, approved the sinking of all merchant ships making use of their radios when stopped. On September 24th, again on Raeder's recommendation, the order protecting French ships was cancelled, and then by stages the need to observe the prize regulations in declared areas was removed, firstly on September 30th in the North Sea, secondly on October 2nd off the British and French coasts in respect of darkened ships, thirdly in waters as far as 15 degrees west, and then on October 19th as far west as 20 degrees. On October 17th U-Boats had already been given permission to attack all ships identified as hostile except liners, and by November 17th even that restriction was removed. Gradually the stage was being set for the all out battle to which Doenitz and the German Naval High Command looked forward.

Meanwhile, the U-Boats had been continuing their operations against undeniably legitimate targets, as and when they were encountered. On September 14th the British aircraft carrier *Ark Royal* was cruising to the west of the Hebrides as part of a U-Boat hunting group. U-39, commanded by Lt-Cdr Glattes, encountered the carrier and he fired off a salvo of torpedoes. They were magnetic pistol models, but unfortunately for Glattes they failed to function as planned, detonated prematurely, and barely damaged *Ark Royal's* paintwork, whereupon her escorting destroyers promptly pounced on U-39, sank it, and captured the crew. But it was a narrow escape for the aircraft carrier.

U-29, in an attack three days later, was more fortunate. Lt-Cdr Schuhardt was lying in wait in the shipping lanes west of the English Channel when he sighted through his periscope a passenger ship of an estimated 10,000 tons. But then an air escort flew into his vision over it and he therefore considered it a legitimate target. Before he could fire his torpedoes, however, the ship turned away and set off on a new course, and since it was steaming too fast for him to follow at his slow underwater speed, he settled down to wait until the ship was out of sight so that he could surface and move round at maximum speed into the favourable frontal position from which to mount an attack. Just before surfacing he took another precautionary look through the periscope, and this time sighted a black smudge on the horizon to port. He looked again more carefully, and when it finally dawned on him that the smudge was in fact an aircraft carrier, he naturally forgot about his plan to hunt the liner. It was about two hours before the carrier came into range, but when she did luck was firmly on Schuhardt's side, for she immediately turned and presented him with the gift target of her vast flank. He seized the opportunity without hesitation and almost by guesswork fired off a salvo of three torpedoes, then crash-dived to evade an approaching destroyer. On the way down two thunderous explosions were heard, followed by another, and then several smaller ones. He could not see it, but he knew that the carrier had been sunk. It was in fact the *Courageous*, and with her went down her commander and 518 of her men.

The destroyers started dropping depth charges, and as Schuhardt took his boat down to 250 feet four heavy explosions shook the conning tower and set the whole boat trembling. But it held intact, and they escaped. Back at base Schuhardt found his exploit the talk of the German navy and nation. It was the first publicised success of

Germany's first success against the Royal Navy; the aircraft carrier 'Courageous' lists before sinking in the Western Approaches

the war by the U-Boat arm, and it served to reaffirm, in professional and public circles, the U-Boat's true capabilities.

If the first successful attack by a U-Boat was a tragic mistake, and the second highly satisfactory, a subsequent one, shortly afterwards, was nothing less than heroic. It was a feat which had been attempted twice by U-Boats at the end of the First World War, and it had ended in the destruction of both. Now Doenitz thought the time was ripe for another try.

The plan was for a U-Boat to penetrate Scapa Flow, and attack the British fleet at its anchorage in the Orkney Islands. It was a project which had been forming in Doenitz's mind since the early days of the war, and intelligence from Naval High Command, together with aerial reconnaissance photographs of obstacles at the various entrances to Scapa Flow, confirmed that an entry into the anchorage by way of the narrow Kirk Sound passage was the most feasible proposition.

Doenitz took great care in choosing the right man for the attempt, and settled on Lt-Cdr Gunther Prien, the captain of U-47 He called Prien for an interview, asked whether he would be willing to undertake the mission, warned him of the hazards, and sent him away to consider his answer for 48 hours. After poring endlessly over all the charts and data, Prien reported back to Doenitz and accepted the task, and to preserve the utmost secrecy, without which the enterprise was bound to fail, Doenitz took the precaution of informing the Commander-in-Chief personally, by word of mouth and not in writing, that the attempt was to be made.

The night chosen was that of October 13th, when both periods of slack water would fall within the hours of darkness, and when the new moon would provide no embarrassing illumination by which U-47 might be located. Prien, like Doenitz, was so keen to preserve secrecy that it was not until the morning of that day, lying on the sea bed within sight of the Orkneys, that he briefed his own crew about the task that faced them. To his relief, they seemed to relish the prospect of this daring but dangerous action, and morale was at its highest. At nightfall Prien surfaced and made for Kirk Sound. The planning had indeed been perfect, and there was no moon, but in one of those uncontrollable eventualities which not even the most accurate and detailed planning can foresee, the night proved to be one of unusual activity on the part of *Aurora Borealis*, and the 'northern lights' lit the sky as if it were daylight. Nevertheless, despite this disadvantage Prien decided to go on, rather than wait for several

HMS 'Royal Oak' sunk by U-47 in a daring operation inside Scapa Flow in October 1939

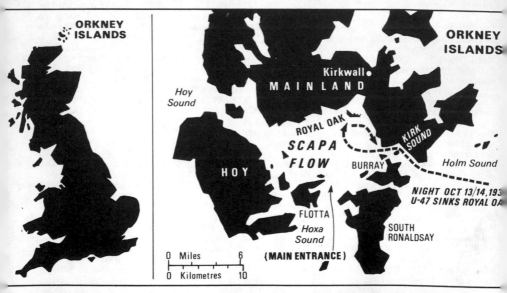

ORKNEY ISLANDS

ORKNEY ISLANDS

Kirkwall•
MAINLAND

Hoy
Sound

ROYAL OAK

SCAPA
FLOW

KIRK SOUND

Holm Sound

HOY

BURRAY

NIGHT OCT 13/14,193
U-47 SINKS ROYAL OA

FLOTTA

SOUTH
RONALDSAY

Hoxa
Sound

(MAIN ENTRANCE)

0   Miles   6
0   Kilometres   10

Scapa Flow, the main British anchorage where Gunther Prien sank the 'Royal Oak'

The brave and brilliant Gunther Prien, Doenitz's favourite U-Boat commander and captain of U-47

weeks until tidal and moon conditions were right again, by which time he might well have lost the edge in terms of both secrecy and morale.

As he navigated towards the sunken ships that blocked Kirk Sound, U-47 was caught by the treacherous tides that flow fast round those islands, and only the most skilful seamanship enabled him to skirt past them. Even so, on the way the boat ran aground and fouled the cable on one of the blockships, but at 12.27 it was through. To the south Prien saw nothing, but to the north, in the main anchorage, his target clearly lay. Two battleships and several destroyers were anchored there. One of the battleships appeared to be of the Royal Oak class, possibly even the *Royal Oak* itself, and the other looked suspiciously like the *Repulse*. Prien went closer, and at 4,000 yards fired three torpedoes from his bow tubes. The fourth misfired. One torpedo struck home against the Royal Oak class ship, which indeed was the *Royal Oak*, but the damage was insignificant, and in extreme disappointment Prien turned away, expecting to be deluged with depth charges from hunting destroyers.

Nothing happened. Astonished at his luck, Prien remained on the surface while his men below worked feverishly to reload the bow torpedo tubes. At 1.16 he went back towards the *Royal Oak* and fired a second salvo. This time the effect was more spectacular. A gigantic explosion threw columns of water and clouds of smoke into the air, and wreckage from the battleship began falling all around the U-Boat.

Thirteen minutes later the *Royal Oak* turned onto her side and sank, with the loss of 24 officers and 809 men.

By now the whole harbour seemed alive with boats searching for the invader. Prien ordered his engineers to produce all the possible power of which their engines were capable, and at top speed they made off for Kirk Sound, leaving behind a thoroughly visible wake of foaming white water which Prien felt sure would be spotted. Surely enough a destroyer raced towards him, sweeping the water with its searchlights, and Prien was certain the end had come. But then, unaccountably, the destroyer turned away and dropped depth charges well behind the U-Boat. They pressed on, clinging to the cover of the coast, where the U-Boat's superstructure merged with the dark background of the mainland. Along the coast road a vehicle drove at high speed, stopped, flashed its lights as if to make a signal, then turned and drove off again in the opposite direction.

Still surging forward as fast as they could go, with the electric motors coupled to the diesels to gain every possible fraction of a knot, they struggled against the fast flowing tide, and eventually reached the narrows of Kirk Sound once more. This time, again with infinite care and considerable skill, Prien steered out between a blockship and the wooden jetty at the southern side of the passage, and finally they vanished.

As it turned out, Prien had done well to carry out his mission on that particular night, for on the following day another old ship, destined to be sunk as an obstruction alongside those already in Kirk Sound, arrived at Scapa Flow. Had it taken its position a day earlier, it is doubtful whether Prien could have successfully negotiated his way in and out of the channel. Meanwhile, the British fleet was hastily moved to alternative anchorages while the defences were further strengthened against future incursions by the U-Boats.

Grand Admiral Raeder was waiting to board the U-Boat as it docked at base. Gratefully he conferred on Prien the award of Iron Cross, First Class, and on all the other members of the crew the Second Class version of that award. There were laurels for Doenitz, too, when the Admiral informed him of his promotion from Kommodore to Rear Admiral, and of his official appointment to the post of Flag Officer, U-Boats (*Befehlshaber der U-boote* or *BdU*). That same day the entire crew was flown off to Berlin for an audience with Hitler. They were national heroes. They had penetrated Scapa Flow, sunk a major unit of the Royal Navy, and escaped. And it was in Scapa Flow, patriotic Germans recalled, that the German fleet had been scuttled at the end of the First World War.

Strike against the convoys

The successes against ships of the Royal Navy were certainly spectacular. But of at least equal importance in the broad context of the war were the operations against Allied merchant shipping, in which the U-Boat commanders carried on their work without the publicity, favourable or otherwise, attached to the exploits of Prien, Schuhardt, and Lemp. Instead of glamour and acclaim, their only reward was the knowledge that every ship they sank was a contribution to the long, slow task of reducing Germany's enemies to submission.

And in those early months, after the comparative peace and security of the training period, the U-Boat crews were having their first taste of what it meant to be at war, of what it was like to be on the receiving end of a depth charge attack from a British escort destroyer.

Lt-Cdr Schultze, who in U-48 eventually won the Knight's Cross as the first commander to sink 100,000 tons of enemy shipping, was among the first to take the full weight of an attack. In an early operation against a pair of freighters sailing under escort, he torpedoed and sank one, then crash dived as a destroyer came racing across to search for him. After lying quietly for half an hour, and apparently eluding the destroyer, he rose to periscope depth, and then to the surface, and this time sighted the perfect target – a full convoy.

In minutes he had its course worked out and was about to submerge for the attack when a Sunderland flying boat appeared, flying straight for him.

Schultze, as commander always the last man to leave the bridge, leaped down the hatch and bawled the order to dive, and as sea water flowed into the ballast tanks and the air hissed out, the U-Boat began to submerge. The nose dipped, and to help the boat on its way all available hands raced forward down the narrow central gangway and crowded into the bows, right up against the torpedo tubes, where their accumulated weight emphasised the boat's downward trim. As the waves closed over the topmost part of the superstructure, the first of four explosions crashed in their ears. The nose dipped even further, and packed into the bows the crew had no way of telling whether the Sunderland's bombs had put them out of control. But at last the trim was righted. There was no serious damage, and it seemed that the U-Boat had escaped this attack, also. Then another sound was heard, the drone of the destroyer's engines as it crept up to them overhead, followed by the sound that injected fear into the hearts of even the bravest U-Boat crew – the 'ping' against the hull that meant the destroyer had found them with its asdic.

It was not long before its first depth charge came down, and the U-Boat shook

Lt -Cdr Schultze in U-48 was the first to achieve his Knight's Cross. On the voyage home a 'mock-up' was forged from cheap metal for the jubilant crew to pin on their commander

under the impact. A second one fell, closer than the first, and again the U-Boat was subjected to its underwater buffeting. Schultze took the boat even deeper, altered course a fraction, and crept forward, using the electric motors sparingly to preserve the maximum possible silence. For twenty minutes nothing happened, and they wondered if they had got off lightly. But no: three more depth charges crashed around them closer than ever to the boat, and wrecked both the depth gauging gear and the telegraphing equipment.

But the pressure hull stood the strain. Schultze decided to go still deeper, right to the bottom, and the U-Boat bumped to rest and lay there, its motors dead, even its auxiliary equipment almost entirely switched off to reduce give-away noise. But it seemed the listeners above had not lost track of it, and the U-Boat crew could hear the noise of the destroyer's engines as it strove to pin-point their position; on and off, on and off, until yet another set of depth charges plunged down on them. Porcelain washbasins and lavatory pedestals were shattered, lightbulbs burst with the shock, and in the conning tower the revolution indicator was smashed. Then again there was silence.

Schultze waited on the bottom until he knew that darkness had fallen overhead, brought his boat up to 200 feet, and at that depth inched forwards for two miles, hoping against hope to surface in a clear sea. His 'clear sea', it turned out, was swarming with escort vessels, twenty-four of them, and he had emerged right in their

midst. Still probing for him, they were creeping forwards for a few yards, then stopping to listen with their asdics, then going on. He made for the biggest gap he could see, that less than a thousand yards wide, and still using the electric underwater motors instead of the noisier surface diesels, and with the rudder under hand control instead of electric, Schultze edged the U-48 out of the jam.

'Disengaged on the surface', he noted with great reserve in his war diary. Then he added triumphantly: 'Got away with it!'

Exploits like that of U-48, although some ended less happily, were typical during the early months of the war, but the toll on enemy shipping was worth all the fear and all the damage, even worth all the U-Boat losses. In September 1939 they sank 41 ships, totalling 153,000 tons, in October 27 ships of 135,000 tons. In November the U-Boats' score fell abruptly to 21 ships of 52,000 tons, and in December remained comparatively low at 25 ships of 81,000 tons.

The reason for the falling off after the first month was simple. As Doenitz had predicted, he would have at any one time only one third of his U-Boats actually in the area of operations, but this did not apply at the beginning of the war, when a total of twenty-three boats were at sea and ready to start their activities simultaneously. It was inevitable that they should all expend their torpedoes and run out of supplies at more or less the same time, and it was some months before they could all settle down to a natural cycle which would leave a consistent number of U-Boats on active operations.

In January the sinkings began to rise once more, with 40 ships of 111,000 tons in that month, and 45 ships of 170,000 tons in February.

Then on March 4th, just as the U-Boats appeared to be getting into their stride again, an inexplicable order was issued preventing further U-Boat sailings, and severely restricting the activities of those already in the vicinity of the Norwegian coast. It was not until the following day that Doenitz himself was put in the picture regarding the reason for this order. Simultaneous landings were to be carried out in Norway and Denmark, and the U-Boats were required to cover the landings against possible counter measures by the Allies.

By withdrawing U-Boats from his training school, and curtailing trials of two new ones, Doenitz was able to compile a force of thirty-one with which to begin the operation. As it turned out, the activities of the U-Boats were almost exclusively confined, during the entire Norwegian campaign, to reconnaisance and transport – hardly the purpose for which they were designed!

But the campaign did at least have its value for the U-Boat arm by showing up at little cost a deficiency which in other

Torpedo strike on an enemy ship. *Bottom* A merchantman goes down. *Right* Survivors are rescued by a Royal Canadian Navy destroyer.

'HMS Nelson', one of Britain's biggest battleships. During the Norwegian campaign she was hit by a torpedo which failed to explode. *Right* Rare air protection for a U-Boat on the high seas

circumstances, against strongly escorted convoys for example, might well have proved expensive. The U-Boats had launched thirty-six attacks, mainly against British transports, but their torpedoes let them down and their failure was total. Prien himself in U-47 sighted six transports of up to 30,000 tons each, disembarking British troops on the evening of April 15th in the narrow waters of Bygdenfiord. Between 10pm and 11pm he fired four torpedoes, at ranges between 750 and 1,500 yards, at a line of transports and destroyers which from his position overlapped to form a solid wall of targets in front of him. It seemed impossible to miss, but not a single torpedo exploded, and the British were not even alerted to his presence. Prien re-loaded, and shortly after midnight went in for a second attack. Both Prien and his first lieutenant personally made a thorough check of all the torpedo adjustments, setting them, as in the first attack, at depths of 12 to 15 feet. This time one torpedo did explode, but that was against a cliff after running off course. It obviously did not the slightest damage to the enemy, but it certainly alerted them to the presence of a U-Boat, and from then on Prien had a hard time. Firstly in turning away he ran aground, and only refloated the boat with extreme difficulty. Then the destroyers pounced on him and subjected him to an onslaught of depth charges. His engines were damaged but he managed to creep away.

Having squeezed out of that tight spot, Prien three days later encountered the battleship *Warspite,* and attacked it with two torpedoes, at a range of only 900 yards. Once more they failed to find the mark, and again one torpedo exploded after running off course, this time at the end of its run, and the destroyers were alerted. They came at U-47 from every direction, and Prien was put in what he reservedly described as 'a most awkward predicament', but again he escaped. On April 20th Prien contacted a third target, this time a convoy steaming north, and although he could easily have attacked, he had by now, not surprisingly, lost confidence in his torpedoes, and he refrained from doing so. When he returned to base he complained, with justification, that he could not be expected to fight with a dummy rifle.

Prien's unhappy failures were symptomatic of a grave general deficiency in the performance of torpedoes during the early months of the war. At the very beginning Lt-Cdr Zahn, in U-56, had come upon the battleships *Rodney, Nelson,* and *Hood,* and ten destroyers. In an operation carried out with great daring against these heavily escorted ships, what might have been a harvest proved a total failure. Zahn fired three torpedoes in a submerged attack, and even heard the bumps as they struck the

sides of the *Nelson.* Yet none exploded. The disappointment so upset Zahn that he had to be withdrawn from active service for a time to become an instructor at the U-Boat school.

By the end of the Norwegian campaign the failure rate had grown to such proportions that an inquiry was instituted into the causes. Some were known to be failing because their magnetic pistols mysteriously malfunctioned in the northern waters off Scandinavia, possibly because of large quantities of iron ore in the region. But Prien's efforts had been with torpedoes carrying contact pistols, so they, it was assumed, had run too deep. The U-Boats appeared to be without an effective weapon.

On April 20th the Torpedo Commission began its investigation into the problem, and exhaustive tests showed several faults, in addition to the causes already recognised. In some cases the striker had failed to fire the charge. In others the initial charge had exploded successfully, but failed to set off the main charge. Occasionally it seemed that torpedoes had struck the target at too acute an angle and not gone off, which may well have been the case in Zahn's unsuccessful brush with the *Nelson.* As a result of the investigation, from June 1940 only contact percussion torpedoes were issued and the unreliable magnetic torpedoes were dropped for a time. But as no greatly improved models even of contact torpedoes were immediately available, the U-Boat commanders were severely limited in their potential sinkings. In several attacks in the following months they found themselves forced to fire more than one torpedo at a vessel which a single shot should have despatched with ease. A subsequent analysis of hits scored by U-Boats showed that only 40 per cent of ships sunk had gone down to a single torpedo. Almost as many had required two hits before they sank, and more than one fifth had required anything up to four torpedoes. U-Boats were thus encountering, on their way back to base, merchant ships against which they could not take the slightest action, having run out of ammunition.

Battle of the Atlantic begins

Following the Norwegian campaign, most of the U-Boats needed repairs and a refit, and several had to be withdrawn from active service to take their place once more in the submarine school, as training vessels for recruits to the expanding U-Boat arm. It was not until June 1940 that U-Boats were available again in any significant numbers for operations against enemy shipping.

Their activities were at first confined to the coastal waters around the British Isles, particularly at the western end of the English Channel, but the German occupation of France in June made available a number of bases on the Atlantic coast in the Bay of Biscay - Lorient, St Nazaire, Brest, La Pallice and Bordeaux. The extreme significance of these ports was thoroughly and gratefully appreciated by the officers of the U-Boat arm. Not only did the boats no longer have to waste time and fuel sailing through vast areas of empty sea on their way to the shipping lanes, but, with the distance from their German bases to the area of operations reduced by some 450 miles, they were able to move further out into the Atlantic, beyond the range of the limited anti-submarine escorts. At that time destroyers sailed only as far as 15 degrees west with a west-bound convoy, where they met an east bound convoy to escort it on the final stages of its journey. The Allies later extended this cover, by moving the meeting point further out into the ocean, to 17 degrees west in July 1940, and 19 degrees west in October 1940. The conflict thus moved out of coastal waters into the wide lonely spaces of the ocean, and inevitably, in the course of time, it came to be known as the Battle of the Atlantic.

In that summer of 1940, the U-Boats, with only weak escorts to contend with, or none at all, were able to put into practice a tactic long advocated by Doenitz, of night attacks on the surface. There the asdic was almost powerless to find them, and their greater surface speed, under diesel engines, made them more than a match for many of the inadequate escort vessels available to the Allies at that time. Moreover, at night in the wastes of the Atlantic, their low superstructure, from the point of view of look outs on the high bridge of a destroyer, allowed them to merge completely into the inky blackness of the ocean without breaking the skyline, and only a lucky strike with a searchlight revealed their position. To the U-Boat commanders, on the other hand, the high structure of a tanker or freighter stood silhouetted high and clear against the lighter background of the night sky, and provided a perfect target. When the U-Boat commanders learned the measure of the escorts, and realised that circumstances were wholly favourable to them, their own daring grew to unprecedented

In the teeth of an Atlantic hurricane,
torpedo attacks were impossible. The
crews could only look to their own safety.

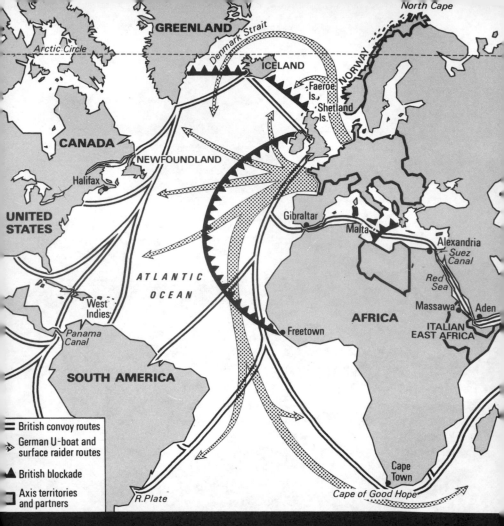

GREENLAND
Arctic Circle
Denmark Strait
ICELAND
North Cape
NORWAY
Faeroe Is.
Shetland Is.
CANADA
NEWFOUNDLAND
Halifax
UNITED STATES
ATLANTIC OCEAN
Gibraltar
Malta
Alexandria
Suez Canal
Red Sea
West Indies
Panama Canal
AFRICA
Massawa
Aden
ITALIAN EAST AFRICA
SOUTH AMERICA
Freetown

≣ British convoy routes
↝ German U-boat and surface raider routes
▲ British blockade
⊐ Axis territories and partners

R. Plate
Cape Town
Cape of Good Hope

German attack routes and the Allied counter measures

Below Two of the U-Boat 'aces' Otto Kretschmer, *left*, was captured by the British, and Joachim Schepke, *right*, was killed by an escort destroyer. *Bottom* Nearing home; one of the few convoys to get through unscathed during the 'happy time'

proportions. Often they penetrated the centre ranks of a convoy itself, and picked off their targets at point blank range.

As the numbers of sinkings rose, this was the golden summer when the famous U-Boat 'aces' made their reputations – Endrass in U-46, Kretschmer in U-99, Schepke in U-100, Frauenheim in U-101, and of course Prien in U-47, who was constantly in there at the fighting.

In June Prien was particularly active, operating mainly alone, and his record for one voyage shows how decisively the U-Boats held the upper hand. On the 14th of the month he sighted through his periscope a convoy of forty-two ships, in seven columns of six each, with only five destroyers as escorts. But they were too fast for him, and he lost contact. Then a straggler steamed into sight – an absolute gift. It took only one torpedo to sink the *Balmoral Wood*, with her cargo of aircraft wings and fuselages. There followed a day without a single sighting, then next morning a convoy of twenty ships appeared, heavily escorted, and with a Sunderland flying boat keeping a keen watch on the waters around them.

Towards nightfall Prien attacked. He ordered one torpedo to be fired, and even before that struck home turned to his second target and fired at that. Then his torpedo artificer was thrown off balance, grabbed at the firing grip to check himself, and a third torpedo accidentally left the tube. The result was three ships on their way to the bottom. Some days later he sank another tanker, then another, until finally he ran out of torpedoes, and was forced to return to base to refuel and refit the U-Boat, and rest the crew before they set out again.

Before the next trip, Hitler facilitated matters by ordering, on August 17th, a total blockade of the British Isles and giving the U-Boats the right to sink neutral shipping on sight, which spelled the end of the fighting according to the 'prize regulations'. On the morning of October 19th Prien contacted another convoy, HX79 bound for Britain, and called in four other boats for the attack – U-38, U-46, U-48, and U-100. That night they accounted for no less than fourteen ships between them, then promptly ran into a second convoy and sank seven more vessels. Together with seventeen ships sunk by another pack of six U-Boats on the preceding night, a total of thirty-eight ships of some 325,000 tons had been accounted for in two days. Prien had by now become the most successful of the U-Boat commanders, and as the first to reach the personal total of 200,000 tons, received the highest possible decoration of the oak leaves to the Knight's Cross.

The amount of shipping sunk during that triumphant summer rose to staggering proportions: in June fifty-eight ships of

Below With survivors on board a U-Boat sails away from a blazing tanker. *Bottom* Into the bag; his craft sunk by depth charges, a German U-Boat hand, wearing his underwater escape equipment, is hauled on board a US Coast Guard Cutter. *Right above* Their vessel sunk, the merchant crew take to the boats to wait for rescue – or start the long row home. *Right below* After a successful hunt, the happy crew reach base again.

284,000 tons, in July thirty-eight ships of
196,000 tons, in August fifty-six ships of
268,000 tons, in September fifty-nine ships
of 295,000 tons, and in October, as the
achievements of the U-Boat arm mounted
to a crescendo, sixty-three ships of 352,000
tons, all with the loss of only six U-Boats.
Small wonder that the months of June to
October 1940 were dubbed by the U-Boat
commanders their 'happy time'.

Apart from the enormous quantities of
shipping sunk, this period was also notable
for its vindication, for the first time in
action, of the principle evolved by Doenitz
out of his experience in the First World
War, that the greatest success was to be
achieved by groups of U-Boats acting in
concert. This method was to be extended,
concentrated on, and developed throughout
the war into the extremely effective 'wolf
pack' tactic. By making contact with a
convoy and keeping it in touch while resist-
ing the temptation to attack alone, one
U-Boat could call up others in the vicinity
for a mass attack, and together they could
inflict losses quite out of proportion to
their own numerical strength. Several
U-Boats attacking together stretched the
escort vessels far beyond their limited
resources, for while the escorts searched
furiously for one U-Boat, others could
frustrate their efforts with attacks on the
other side of the convoy or even from
within its columns. In addition the U-Boat
commanders soon realised that once one
ship had been sunk, at least one of the
escorts would be obliged to fall back behind
the convoy to pick up survivors, making
the work of the U-Boats even easier. Or
alternatively, one of the merchantmen
would itself fall back to help a stricken
comrade, presenting an easy target to the
lurking U-Boats.

To keep up the constant flow of
information and communication between
the U-Boats and base, which was essential
to maintain the arm at peak efficiency,
Doenitz set up at his headquarters in
France a 'situations room' where all
possible intelligence on enemy ship movements was translated into the form of wall
charts. Other charts showed relevant
navigational data such as the state of
tides, weather conditions, and details of
different time zones. With this complete
picture of the situation at sea, Doenitz
could move his packs into the best possible
position in which to intercept convoys.

The 'happy time' was an apt description
of that fruitful summer, and it had been
achieved with no more than fifty-seven
U-Boats in commission at any time. What
might have happened had Doenitz had his
300!

**Heading for action on the convoy routes,
a submarine makes good speed on the
surface.**

The problems mount: Winter 1941

Inevitably, the happy time came to an end.

In the months from November 1940, a great deal of refitting was necessary, and the number of boats available for operations was severely diminished, causing a cut in the numbers of sinkings for November, for example, to thirty-two ships of 147,000 tons. In addition, a number of other factors combined to reduce the effectiveness of those few U-Boats which were still operational. Simplest of all was the autumn change in the weather, which that year brought exceptionally bad Atlantic storms. As the weather deteriorated, the small U-Boats were tossed about like barrels on the waves, the seas broke over the conning towers, and the officers and ratings on the bridge watch were compelled to tie themselves to the boats to prevent being washed overboard. In such conditions, and with waves and spray to obscure the vision of lookouts and make their task doubly difficult, the sighting of convoys became more and more rare.

Moreover, towards the end of 1940, as the threat of invasion of the British Isles by German forces receded, many of the boats which that threat had kept tied down were released to play an increasing part in the protection of convoys in the Atlantic. This again forced the U-Boats to move further into the wider expanses of the ocean where convoys were less well protected, and with greater areas to search, the incidence of sightings was still further reduced. During the whole of December only one convoy was encountered, and in a night attack on the surface Schultze, Kretschmer, and two others torpedoed and sank ten merchant vessels, plus the armed cruiser *Forfar*. But one sighting, however impressive its results, was far from sufficient, and it was only lucky sightings of ships sailing independently that kept the U-Boats' performance for December up to thirty-seven ships of 213,000 tons.

The escort forces were also augmented by the acquisition, from America, of fifty old destroyers, in exchange for the use by the United States of air bases on British territory in the West Indies and British Guiana. Furthermore, the British achieved considerable co-operation between the navy and the air force, and convoys were beginning to come under the protection of aircraft, particularly Sunderland flying boats, from Coastal Command. With their airborne depth charges they could force a U-Boat in contact with a convoy to submerge, which not only slowed its speed, but also rendered it 'blind'. If the aircraft kept the U-Boat down for long enough the convoy's course could be changed, and contact would be lost.

On December 4th, operational control of British Coastal Command was ordered to be taken over by the Admiralty, and although Coastal Command remained part

Devastation for a lurking U-Boat: the explosive effect of a destroyer depth charge

Above Air attack against a U-Boat; a Whitley releases its depth charges. *Below* Long range bomber and its U-Boat colleague; an unusual moment when their paths coincided

of the Royal Air Force, the Admiralty at least had the major voice in deciding how its aircraft were to be used, with the result that convoy protection from the air improved greatly during the early days of 1941.

Admiral Doenitz, by contrast, was experiencing extreme difficulty in obtaining any kind of co-operation with the Luftwaffe. Grand Admiral Raeder had had long and bitter pre-war arguments with Goering on the needs of the navy for an integrated naval air arm independent of the German Air Force, and lost. Now war was a reality, Doenitz saw clearly that his U-Boats were wholly inadequate to the task of carrying out their own reconnaissance. Being specifically designed to squat low in the water, even a watch with binoculars situated at the highest possible point of the conning tower enjoyed only a limited range of vision. And with no air reconnaissance,

able to scout vast areas and home the U-Boat packs onto a sighted convoy, the U-Boats were inevitably condemned to waiting, often for weeks on end, until a convoy should fortuitously run into their path.

In December 1940 Doenitz sent a memorandum to Naval High Command explaining in convincing detail the need for organised air reconnaissance specifically under the control of the U-Boat arm. On January 2nd 1941 Doenitz saw Raeder in Berlin and elaborated on the memorandum to him. Raeder was of the same opinion as Doenitz, and arranged for Doenitz to have an interview the following day with the Chief of Staff at Supreme Headquarters, General Jodl. Jodl was also deeply impressed with the force of Doenitz's arguments, and passed the message on to Hitler. Doenitz was well pleased. On January 7th Hitler personally ordered a group of Focke-Wulf

Kondor long range aircraft stationed at Bordeaux to be lopped off Goering's air force and allocated to the U-Boat arm.

All these negotiations took place without Goering's knowledge – he was on leave at the time on a hunting trip. But he learned of the move immediately on his return and a clash seemed inevitable. On February 7th Goering invited Doenitz to visit him in his headquarters train in which he was travelling close to Doenitz's French command post. There Doenitz refused to connive with Goering in having the order rescinded, turned down an invitation to dinner, and left in the iciest of atmospheres.

The aircraft, which Doenitz hoped would come immediately into the picture by homing U-Boats directly on to the convoys, proved less than equal to the task. Their range was inadequate, there were insufficient of them to cover large areas in an organised search, and their navigating skill proved so inaccurate that the U-Boats failed to find a convoy even when large packs of them converged and saturated the area in which the aircraft had reported it. Ironically, the first example of co-operation between the aircraft and the U-Boats occurred when U-37 encountered a convoy homeward bound to Britain from Gibraltar, and with long wave radio signals homed the aircraft onto it from 150 miles away for a successful bomb attack. It was the exact reverse of the way the inter-service co-operation was designed to work. Many months passed before experience and training brought the air crews to the pitch where they could play a full and really useful part in the operations of the U-Boat arm.

Developments in the technical field also served to cut back the advantage which the U-Boats held over the escorts. Firstly the British developed accurate radio direction finding apparatus which to a great extent countered the effectiveness of the wolf pack tactics. Receivers on land and in ships at sea were able to pick up and pin-point the signals sent by a U-Boat to bring others to the scene, and long before they arrived the escorts would be on their way to attack it, force it under, and at least break the contact, if not sink it outright.

In making full use of signals picked up in this way, and of any other information, the British matched Doenitz's 'situations room' with their own 'submarine tracking room' at the Admiralty in London. There every scrap of intelligence was incorporated into charts and maps, all brought continually up to date, from which it was possible to gain a complete picture of the positions of wolf packs and the likely movements of individual U-Boats. Then if a convoy appeared to be sailing into danger, it could be swiftly re-routed to frustrate the German effort.

In the vital field of radar, a comparison — between British and German experience again shows how different was their spirit of enterprise. When all its manifestations accumulated, it must have been a critical factor in the eventual outcome of the war. In January 1941 the first of a new kind of radar set, smaller and less cumbersome than its predecessors, was fitted into aircraft of Coastal Command and into some of the escort vessels. The aircraft were thus able to contribute to the hunt for U-Boats at night, when most of the attacks were made, as well as by day. The escort vessels benefited by having a means of locating a surfaced U-Boat, which was immune to the asdic, and they could then either ram it on the surface, or force it below, where the asdic would again come into its own and depth charges could be dropped.

While the British were thus exploiting their technical skills, Germany was lagging behind. Since 1935 Germany had possessed radar sets in the half-metre wavelength, but German scientists were unnecessarily sceptical about its potential for further development, and had failed to explore the possibilities of a short wave length radar set. Then in 1940 and 1941 Hitler himself had aggravated the effect of that error by halting all development in the radar field, and by the time British progress became evident, the Germans had been taken completely off their guard and it was doubtful whether they could catch up.

Early in 1941 the British were able to make the best possible use of their newly acquired radar when they started to fly patrols from air bases in Iceland, which had been occupied in the previous year. This was the first stage in the process which the Allies regarded as one of their most important aims, the closing of the 'air gap' – the area between the limits of shorebased aircraft on each side of the Atlantic where the U-Boats held the advantage. A similar 'air gap' existed in the region of the Azores and Canaries, where northbound convoys from Sierra Leone and Gibraltar were outside the limits of air cover. By stages, as more aircraft of a longer range became available, the Allies succeeded in reducing these gaps and making operations for the U-Boats correspondingly more difficult and restricted.

The gradual introduction of these factors kept down sinkings by the U-Boats to twenty-one ships of 127,000 tons in January, and thirty-nine ships of 197,000 tons in February. Their successes were mainly achieved among stragglers which had either refused to take part in a convoy, or had fallen behind and no longer came under the effective protection of the escorts, which of course were obliged to stay close to the convoy where the majority of their charges were sailing. Some success was also achieved by U-Boats which Doenitz, under considerable pressure and with great

49

reservations, agreed to divert from their attacks on the northern convoy routes, to the South Atlantic. Some of them were able to reap a reasonable harvest off Freetown, Sierra Leone, but Doenitz still did not consider their use in that area fully justified. He regretted taking away from the northern convoy routes valuable 'eyes', whose sightings might have brought more U-Boats into play and restored the figures for ships sunk to those achieved during the climactic summer of 1940.

The difficulties which U-Boats operations were undergoing in the early months of 1941 were epitomised in three events which occurred within a few days in March. The U-Boat packs in the North Atlantic were ordered to congregate in the area to the south of Iceland, where Doenitz believed they would run into convoys. Doenitz was right. It was Prien, at the centre of the battle as always, who sighted and reported convoy OB293 steaming to the northwest. Other U-Boats closed in, and in attacks after dark they sank two ships and damaged two others. But the destroyers were unusually active. The old boat UA was so badly damaged by depth charges that its commander Eckerman had to disengage and sail straight for base. U-70 was sunk after Matz, its commander, and most of his crew surrendered. Otto Kretschmer, in U-99, was also driven off with only half his torpedoes fired. Prien dropped back and continued to shadow the convoy, and at 4.24am on March 7th he reported its position. Shortly afterwards, the destroyer *Wolverine*, under Commander J M Rowland, tore down on U-47 and depth charged it as it crash dived. The propellor was damaged, and from then on it gave out a persistent and fatal rattle which kept *Wolverine's* crew in easy contact. A new set of depth charges was dropped, and the debris which floated to the surface confirmed their accuracy. There were no survivors. That day, when Doenitz's command post broadcast an order to all U-Boats to report their position, U-47 was among those that failed to reply. A specific call to U-47 to report its position produced no response, and as the day went by, hope faded. Doenitz himself dictated the obituary notice to the hero of Scapa Flow. Although Supreme Command kept Prien's death secret from the German people until May, Doenitz's gesture was a measure of the esteem and personal affection in which he held one of his first and most successful U-Boat commanders.

Prien's sinkings at the time of his death, twenty-eight ships of 160,000 tons, were matched by the work of only two other commanders. Joachim Schepke in U-100 had thirty-nine ships of 159,130 tons to his credit, and standing alone and far above either of their achievements were those of Otto Kretschmer in U-99, with a personal tally of no less than forty-four merchant

Admiral Doenitz awards the Iron Cross to a U-Boat crew

ships and a destroyer totalling 266,629 tons.

Both Kretschmer and Schepke were in the pack which made contact with the fast convoy HX112. On the night of March 16th, shortly before dusk, three destroyers spotted U-100 lurking on the horizon and raced off to deal with it. The convoy's protective screen, thus broken, allowed Kretschmer to move in and set to work among the columns of ships, and he sank five. Their frantic signals, and the inevitable glow of the flames, drew the destroyers once more to the convoy, and Schepke, relieved of their unwelcome attentions, was able to catch up. But at 3.00am he was found again by the destroyers, and a set of depth charges forced U-100 to the surface. The destroyer *Vanoc* rammed and sank the boat, and Schepke himself, standing between the bridge and the periscope, was crushed and killed by *Vanoc's* bows.

Kretschmer's U-99, half an hour later, was picked up on the asdic of the destroyer *Walker*, which dropped depth charges and forced it, too, to the surface. Kretschmer and most of his crew surrendered and were rescued by the destroyer, and soon afterwards U-99 sank.

These losses, of three of the most successful and daring U-Boat commanders, within the space of little more than a week, came as a grievous blow to the U-Boat arm, and a bitter personal shock to Doenitz, who had always made a point, as a principle of his leadership, of establishing a close contact with his subordinate officers. In the overall picture, their deaths foretold the end of the concept of U-Boat 'aces', and the extension and formalisation of the 'wolf pack' tactic which was already showing itself, in the face of developing British escort techniques, to be the only feasible basis for future U-Boat operations.

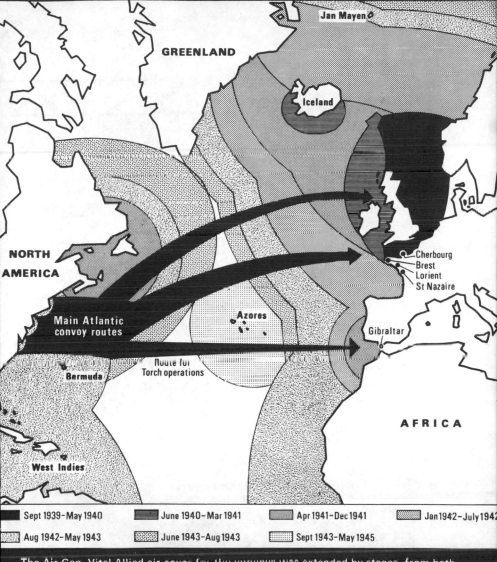

GREENLAND

Jan Mayen

Iceland

NORTH
AMERICA

Cherbourg
Brest
Lorient
St Nazaire

Main Atlantic
convoy routes

Azores

Gibraltar

Route for
Torch operations

Bermuda

AFRICA

West Indies

Sept 1939–May 1940   June 1940–Mar 1941   Apr 1941–Dec 1941   Jan 1942–July 1942

Aug 1942–May 1943   June 1943–Aug 1943   Sept 1943–May 1945

The Air Gap. Vital Allied air cover for the convoys was extended by stages, from both
sides of the Atlantic, until the 'gap' was finally closed

Convoy at sea; the boat at centre right
has just been torpedoed

52

The battle area grows: Summer 1941

During the summer months of 1941, Doenitz's efforts were continually thwarted by orders to withdraw some of his U-Boats from operations against Allied shipping in the Atlantic and make them available for duties of various kinds elsewhere. The air force, in their need for long distance weather information, claimed two U-Boats which were permanently occupied in radioing reports, and this, at a time when Doenitz was down to four operational boats, effectively reduced his resources by fifty per cent. In July, after the outbreak of war with Russia, up to six boats were detached from the Atlantic fleet for early operations in the Arctic, and since there was as yet no convoy shipping against which they could exercise their proven techniques, they patrolled the vast wastes of the empty ocean in frustration and boredom.

Then there were their own escort duties. In what Doenitz regarded, quite properly, as a fundamental misconception of their only effective role by the political leadership, U-Boats were called on to escort auxiliary cruisers, supply ships, and captured prize vessels. U-Boats were designed as hunt and strike vessels. As defensive weapons, facing either diving aircraft or ships which could attack with long range shell-fire, the diminutive U-Boats were conspicuously ill-armed and under-equipped. Experience by now had shown that the

loss of a single U-Boat from a patrolling pack, particularly in view of the failure of the Focke-Wulfs yet to take their proper part in the pattern of reconnaissance and reporting, depleted the capabilities of the group as a whole far more seriously than its numerical significance indicated. When their number dwindled, the U-Boats could neither locate nor maintain contact with a convoy with sufficient certainty, nor could they attack in sufficient strength, to baffle the efforts of an active escort group.

Finally, in September 1941, six U-Boats from the Atlantic passed through the Straits of Gibraltar into the Mediterranean to support Rommel in his campaign in North Africa. The Italian supply fleet to the Afrika Korps was then being decimated by the Royal Navy, and Rommel's troops were in dire danger of being left without supplies. The introduction of the U-Boats, and their reinforcement in November by four more, brought immediate short term relief. On November 13th U-81 attacked and torpedoed the aircraft carrier *Ark Royal* and after listing for more than twelve hours, during which all but one of her crew were taken off, she sank. Several days later the battleship *Barham* was sunk by U-331, and on December 14th U-557 accounted for the cruiser *Galatea*. The move of some U-Boats to the Mediterranean might have been necessary, and indeed was successful, but at the end of November Hitler's en-

A keen watch for the first speck on the horizon

HMS 'Barham', torpedoed in the Mediterranean, was the U-Boat's sole British battleship victim on the high seas. 859 men died when the magazine exploded

Another capital ship goes down. The aircraft carrier 'Ark Royal', missed several times during the war, was finally sunk in the Mediterranean. Her Swordfish aircraft, unable to take off because of the list, went down with her. *Right* During a pause in the fight, the U-Boat crew reload their anti-aircraft gun

thusiasm for the Mediterranean theatre, and his basic lack of interest in or understanding of what was going on in the wider oceans, led him to station ten U-Boats in the eastern Mediterranean, and fifteen more in the immediate vicinity of Gibraltar. For the Allies, this meant instant relief of their shipping in the Atlantic, and as they quickly woke up to the strengthening of U-Boat forces in this area, they promptly set about fortifying their defences at Gibraltar. Two disadvantages accrued for the U-Boats. Firstly, owing to their closeness to land, they were forced to stay submerged for most of the time to avoid being sighted by the heavy anti-submarine sea and air patrols: they could thus move only with the excruciating slowness allowed by their electric motors, unable to hunt for targets, and able to see only as far as their limited periscope range allowed. Secondly, the tidal conditions in the Straits of Gibraltar, which caused a strong and steady current to run from west to east out of the Atlantic and into the Mediterranean, presented one almost insuperable problem to the U-Boats. With the aid of the current, it was comparatively easy, at least before the British strengthened their anti-submarine measures, for a U-Boat to enter the

Mediterranean. Once their presence in force there had been discovered, it was virtually impossible for them to struggle out again. They could make but slow progress against the tidal stream, and the length of their extended passage gave the ever-alert defences ample time to discover and deal with them. Excluded for ever from any further part outside the Mediterranean, these U-Boats were, as Doenitz himself put it, in a mousetrap.

Partly as a result of this unhappy meddling with the unity of the U-Boat arm, wherein lay its great strength, sinkings during the summer of 1941 showed a drastic fall; after successes in May (fifty-eight ships of 325,000 tons) and June (sixty-one ships of 310,000 tons), achievements tailed off to twenty-two ships of 94,000 tons in July, and twenty-three ships of 80,000 tons in August. September brought an encouraging if temporary upsurge in the number of ships sunk, largely as a consequence of Doenitz's characteristically impeccable reasoning. He argued that the meagre pickings of July and August were accountable not to any failure on the part of the few U-Boats left in the Atlantic or their crews, but to the re-routing of the convoys far to the north after they had

58

59

Type VIIC

The 'VII' series of U boats were the most
prolific in the North Atlantic. The record
for shipping sunk in the Battle of the
Atlantic was held by U.99 (ex U.69), a
Type VII b commanded by Otto Kretschmer.

Displacement
769/871 tons
Dimensions
$220\frac{1}{4} \times 20\frac{1}{4} \times 15\frac{3}{4}$ feet
Machinery
2-shaft diesel/electric motors, BHP/SHP
$2,800/750 = 17/7\frac{1}{2}$ knots
Bunkers and radius
OF 114 tons; 6,500/80 miles at 12/4 knots
Armament
One 3.5-inch, one 37 mm AA, two 20 mm
AA (2 ×1) guns; five 21-inch torpedo tubes
(four foward and one aft — fourteen
torpedoes or fourteen mines)
Complement
44

passed Newfoundland. When the convoys moved north to take advantage of the air cover offered by Hudson and Sunderland squadrons flying from Iceland, Doenitz moved his wolf packs with them, and surely enough his decision was justified by events. On September 11th a slow eastbound convoy, SC42, was sighted close to the Greenland coast. It consisted of sixty-four ships, and, though the U-Boats had no such detailed knowledge at the time, was carrying a total of more than half a million tons of cargo. Whatever its contents, a convoy of sixty-four ships was a welcome target after the disappointments of the preceding weeks, and the U-Boats started to congregate. The now familiar exchange of radio signals, picked up and interpreted by either side, led to a re-routing of the convoy even further to the north, but evasion was impossible. On the morning of September 9th the captain of a merchantman which had unwisely fallen behind was treated to that sinister and terrifying sight, the tip of a periscope poking from the depths to reconnoitre the prospect above. That night, shortly after the moon rose at 9.30pm, the first ship was sunk. Before midnight four U-Boats had gathered and were at work, some within the columns of the convoy, and eight ships had gone down. Four more U-Boats appeared, and the outnumbered escorts, a mere three corvettes and a Canadian destroyer, were reduced to chasing helplessly in and out among the ships. After midnight, with two more ships destroyed, the escorts located a submerged U-Boat, and gathered to attack. But the convoy moved on, and with other U-Boats threatening, the escorts were compelled to abandon their hunt and quickly catch up. Safety, for this U-Boat as for all others, lay in numbers, and the wolf pack idea proved its worth in defence, as well as in attack.

On the night of September 10th, the torpedoing began again, and seven more ships were sunk. By now the convoy's calls for help had led to the arrival of two more escort corvettes – small comfort for the convoy since one of the original escort had already been detached to tow a tanker to Iceland. But the new ships were quickly in action, and soon after they arrived they tracked down and sank U-510. The next day other escorts arrived, including two destroyers, the Veteran and Leamington, which sank U-207. Then fog came down, and the U-Boats, which with their delicate structure could not afford to risk even an accidental ramming, were forced to withdraw.

This success on the northern route was accompanied by others in September. Four ships were sunk from an eastbound convoy in the western Atlantic, then four more were sunk in the north Atlantic from a convoy of eleven en route from Freetown

to Britain, and finally a convoy from Gibraltar, escorted by ten destroyers and corvettes, was spotted by an aircraft of Doenitz's air arm, coming into its own at last. It led the U-Boats to the scene, and they sank nine ships. Thus the September total rose to fifty-three ships of 202,000 tons.

For the remainder of the year, there was a lull in U-Boat activity. Many boats were diverted from the main arena. Others enjoyed indifferent luck and after thirty-two ships of 157,000 tons in October, only thirteen ships of 62,000 tons were sunk in November, the lowest total since May of the preceding year.

A novel British development contributed to the lull when they provided a certain amount of air cover in the 'gap' by fitting catapult flight decks, in the autumn of 1941, to some merchant ships. These new 'Catapult Aircraft Merchantmen', or CAM ships, carried a single Hurricane fighter which after it had been flown off had to be ditched in the sea while the pilot took his chance by bailing out, parachuting alongside the merchantman, and hoping to be picked up. In most cases the exercise was successful.

During November, the poor sinkings of the U-Boats themselves were accompanied by further misfortune to two of their supply ships. After an exceptionally successful cruise in the Atlantic, Pacific, and Indian oceans, with twenty-two ships sunk to her credit, the cruiser Atlantis arrived at a rendezvous on November 22nd to refuel U-126. While the U-Boat Commander, Lt-Cdr Bauer, was on the cruiser making arrangements for the refuelling, aircraft catapulted off the British cruiser Devonshire sighted these two ships. Devonshire opened fire and Atlantis blew up and sank. Because of the presence of the U-Boat, the Devonshire did not remain behind to take on survivors, and U-126 was left with the task of looking after the captain of the Atlantis and about 100 other men. A second supply ship, Python, was ordered to meet U-126 and take on the Atlantis survivors from their lifeboats. By November 25th they were safely on board, but on December 1st the British cruiser Dorsetshire encountered Python and sank her. Four U-Boats in the area took on board between them no less than 414 survivors from Python and Atlantis, and in impossibly cramped conditions they set course across the equator for home. Four Italian submarines joined in the rescue work near the Cape Verde Islands, and by the end of January all the survivors were safely in the Biscay bases after a journey of 5,000 miles.

In December 1941 the numbers of U-Boats in operation was down to twelve off Gibraltar, and fifteen covering the rest of the Atlantic. In the circumstances it is hardly surprising that U-Boat sinkings for the month in the North Atlantic amounted

Ingenious answer to the U-Boat peril; a Hurricane fighter, catapulted from an adapted merchantman, sets out to search for U-Boats

to only nine ships, of 46,000 tons. British escort work from Gibraltar was developing in strength and the auxiliary aircraft carrier *Audacity* was harrying the U-Boats and severely curtailing their activities. The British assembled an especially strong escort for the Gibraltar convoy HG76, which sailed on December 14th. With *Audacity* in the escort were two sloops, three destroyers, and seven corvettes, and in command was a British sailor who was to become well known as a most successful escort leader and a thorn in the side of the U-Boat arm, Commander F J Walker in the sloop *Stork*. The fighting started soon after the convoy had sailed. First two U-Boats trying to pass through the Straits of Gibraltar were attacked from the air, and the next day, December 15th, U-127 was sunk by a destroyer. But on the 16th nine U-Boats closed in on the convoy, and, despite the incessant air cover, kept up a constant attack throughout the coming days and nights. By December 17th the convoy had steamed out of reach of the Gibraltar-based air escort but not yet into range of aircraft based in England, and the U-Boat pack and escort group were able to test their mettle against each other. The outcome was not a happy one for the Germans. On December 17th U-31 (Lt-Cdr Baumann) was sunk in a duel with both the surface escorts and Marletts flown off the *Audacity*. On the 18th U-434 (Lt-Cdr Heyda) was sunk by the surface escort, and on the following day Commander Walker himself in *Stork* located and sank U-574. On December 21st the U-Boat arm suffered one of its most grievous losses when the surface escort sank U-567, which was commanded by Lt-Cdr Endrass, who was one of the last surviving 'aces' had been among the best known and most successful commanders. On the other side of the 'balance sheet' the U-Boats achieved the valuable

feat of sinking the *Audacity* on December 21st, and the destroyer *Stanley* was also sent to the bottom, but from the convoy itself the U-Boats had only succeeded in sinking two merchant ships. At the expense of five of their own numbers destroyed, this had proved an expensive operation. On December 23rd aircraft from the Royal Air Force bases in England started to appear over the convoy and again forced the U-Boats to seek shelter below the surface, and by this time Doenitz had no alternative but to call off the attacks.

After what amounted to resounding defeat he was forced to think carefully about the activities of his U-Boat arm in the face of developing defence techniques on the part of the escort forces. With his usual unshakable tenacity Doenitz refused to accept the evidence of a single operation as a basis for altering U-Boat tactics. He remained convinced that attacks on convoys were still the most profitable deployment of his forces. HG76 had after all enjoyed a particularly strong escort, and had sailed in calm weather, which was never favourable to the U-Boats.

For the time being, he planned to go on forming his U-Boats into 'wolf packs' and sending them out to hunt for convoys. But then in December a new factor had entered the war which in the coming months was to exert a considerable influence on the course of the U-Boat operations. On the 7th of the month Japanese aircraft had attacked and virtually destroyed the United States Pacific Fleet at anchor in Pearl Harbour, and when on December 11th the German government formally declared war on the United States, new opportunities immediately arose for the U-Boats, which for the time being were to push into the background the fierce and absorbing struggle which was developing in the North Atlantic.

Operations in American waters: January to July 1942

While the official German declaration of war against the United States of America took place on December 11th 1941, it did not imply any sudden and wholly new antagonism between these two adversaries. The Japanese attack on Pearl Harbour, it is true, which directly precipitated the declaration of hostilities by the Germans, came as a complete surprise to German High Command. But as is the way with wars, incidents had been taking place in the preceding months which had drawn the United States inexorably into the conflict.

The American government had made large quantities of arms available to the British long before war broke out, and this policy was only dropped in 1937 when the Neutrality Act banned the export of arms and financial credits to belligerents. That desire for neutrality did not last long, however, and in November 1939 the Act was repealed. In its place the 'Cash and Carry' system was introduced, which permitted the supply of arms to any belligerent, providing he could pay for them in cash and take them away in his own ships. It sounded perfectly fair, though it applied only to the Allies, who had command of the sea, and was of no value to the German cause, since none of their merchantmen could use the high seas and risk running the gauntlet of British maritime power.

President Roosevelt, furthermore, in July 1940 declared it his intention to give Britain all aid short of war. Later that month arrangements were made for the transfer of the fifty obsolete destroyers from the American Navy to the British convoy escort forces, which even Churchill admitted was in direct contravention of the principles of neutrality and would have justified the Germans in declaring war on the United States there and then.

The American fiction of preserving neutrality was not aided by the arrival in London, in August 1940, of a delegation from the United States Navy led by Admiral R L Ghormley, and composed some of the most capable members of his staff.

Their mission was to glean from the British Admiralty, who were more than willing to involve the United States in the war by supplying it to them, as much knowledge and information as could be supplied after nearly a year of experience in conducting maritime warfare. The mission learned a great deal about British methods and theories, and about their latest radar developments, and Admiral Ghormley was able to report back that he had obtained, fresh from the laboratories of war, information of priceless value to national defence.

Nor were Roosevelt's policies regarding shipping calculated to encourage the Germans in any belief they may have entertained that the United States would not one day be numbered among their enemies. In September 1939, immediately after Britain's declaration of war against Germany, Roosevelt had formulated a 'security zone' many miles out into the Atlantic and ordered patrols of American warships to preserve its neutrality by keeping ships of belligerent nations outside its limits. Despite their official neutrality, American warships had also, from the very beginning, reported the positions of German merchant vessels to the British. In February 1941 the 'security zone' extended to 26 degrees west and only 740 sea miles from the coast of Europe, and in July still further to 22 degrees west, to coincide with the occupation by United States troops of Iceland which the new security zone covered.

Hitler's policy during these ominous months was to avoid as far as possible any incident which might lead to an opening of hostilities with a new and powerful adversary. In September 1939 he issued an order to the German Naval High Command forbidding any incident involving ships of the United States. It was a difficult policy for the German Navy to pursue, although until the summer of 1941 the task of distinguishing between ships of one country and another before making an attack was largely simplified by the Americans' determination to avoid the blockade area around the British Isles where German U-Boats were operating. Then on June 20th 1941 the United States battleship *Texas* appeared in this area. U-203 spotted her and attacked with torpedoes, but missed, and was fortunate to remain undetected.

To comply with Hitler's wishes, Doenitz issued an order to U-Boat commanders insisting that all targets should be positively identified as hostile before an attack was made. In this way the appearance of the *Texas* in British blockade waters provided for some time the perfect protection to all vessels of the Royal Navy, for by the time a U-Boat commander had come close enough, and had waited long enough, to make sure of a positive identification, he had generally been detected and attacked by destroyers. Later orders to the U-Boat captains permitted retaliation against any attacking ships, but only after the attack had begun, and once a pursuer was shaken off, they were still not allowed to return for a counter attack. The U-Boat was reduced to cruising about the ocean with so many restrictions it could hardly begin to operate.

But in this testing atmosphere incidents could not be permanently avoided. On September 4th 1941 the United States destroyer *Greer* earned the distinction of being the first American vessel to fire a shot in anger at a U-Boat. Acting on the report of a British aircraft, the *Greer* located and shadowed U-652. *Greer*, as was then the practice, kept in contact with the U-Boat

with its asdic, and put out a continual radio report of its position to any Allied destroyer or aircraft which might be able to take advantage. A second British aircraft arrived on the scene and dropped four depth charges, but they all missed. Two hours later the U-Boat fired a torpedo at the *Greer*, which also missed. The destroyer counter-attacked, and it, too, missed. Shortly afterwards contact was lost, and the destroyer and U-Boat went their separate ways. No blood was shed, but indignation among the American people at the attack on their destroyer was rife, and on September 15th it was announced that the United States Navy had been ordered to capture or destroy all Axis commerce raiders. They were regarded as 'pirates' From that time on a situation of 'undeclared war' existed between Germany and the United States.

It was in September 1941, also, that American ships took over the escort duties of convoys sailing between Newfoundland and Iceland, with the justification that they were protecting shipping between two United States bases in order to supply troops in Argentina and Iceland.

Even so, in the face of strong protests from Grand Admiral Raeder himself, Hitler was constant in his policy towards the United States, and refused to withdraw the order to U-Boats to take defensive measures only.

The 'undeclared war' was not without its incidents, inevitable while American vessels were involved in escorting convoys out of Newfoundland. On October 10th a U-Boat attacked the convoy SC48, and torpedoed the United States destroyer *Kearney* which was on escort duty. *Kearney* stayed afloat, but a similar attack against the convoy HX156 on October 31st resulted in the sinking by a U-Boat of the United States destroyer *Reuben James* – the first United States loss in the Battle of the Atlantic.

In the circumstances, it is hardly surprising that after Japan and the United States entered into open hostilities on December 7th, Hitler should at last remove, on December 9th, all restrictions on U-Boat operations against American ships, and should follow this order two days later with the declaration of war. War with the United States thus developed as a crystallisation of events: its declaration was a mere formality.

After the lull in the North Atlantic during the preceding months, the opportunity to attack American shipping in American waters was an inviting prospect to Doenitz and his U-Boat commanders. The Americans, despite the visit of their mission to pick the brains of the British, had no practical experience of how to combat the operations of a U-Boat pack, and until the passing weeks allowed them to organise their defences and group their

The bows of a U-Boat. *Below* Raeder, Doenitz and Hitler review the men

A torpedo explosion directly below the
hull was enough to snap a ship in two

merchant ships into the mutually protective convoys under naval and air escort, the western waters of the Atlantic ocean promised plentiful pickings for the U-Boat arm. Accordingly, Doenitz proposed the immediate despatch there of twelve U-Boats, including six large Type IXC boats which were at present engaged in the Gibraltar area, but which with their greater fuel and armaments capacity would obviously be better employed on the longer range operations. He was becoming accustomed to having his requests turned down. This was no exception.

Between December 16th and 25th, five U-Boats put out from the Biscay ports to cross the Atlantic for operation *Paukenschlag* (roll on the kettle drums), Germany's first blow against American shipping. It was the full extent of the force available from an operational arm at that time no less than ninety-one strong. Of these, twenty-three were trapped in the Mediterranean or on their way there, six were off Gibraltar, and four were off Norway. Of the remainder over half were in the dockyards either being or waiting to be repaired, and half of the score at sea were *en route* to or from operations.

The five commanders set out in great good heart, and in mid-January arrived at the area designated for their opening attack, between the Gulf of St Lawrence and Cape Hatteras. Their optimism was well-founded, for the Americans had taken even less defensive measures than they had expected. Shipping was sailing with its normal peacetime lighting. Towns along the coast were bright with lights, and lighthouses and buoys still shone out their invaluable information. Merchant ships kept their 600 metre wave bands while the operators talked incessantly about every kind of topic, including details of their positions, and the defence forces communicated by radio details of destroyer sailing schedules, aircraft patrols, and rescue work in progress, all of which was intercepted by the U-Boat commanders and put to excellent use. The result was utter holocaust. By day the U-Boats lay still on the bottom some distance from the shipping routes. At night they approached the coast submerged, surfaced in the middle of the shipping routes, and wrought havoc on a grand scale among the unsuspecting merchantmen.

Before the five boats left that operational area they had sunk ships to an extent never encountered since the end of the 'happy time' in the North Atlantic – tallies amounting to eight ships of 53,000 tons (Lt-Cdr Hardegen in U-123), five ships of 50,000 tons (Lt-Cdr Zapp in U-66), four ships of 31,000 tons (Lt-Cdr Kals in U-130). In his war diary Hardegen recorded the lament that there were not more U-Boats in the region. 'If only there had been ten or twenty boats,' he wrote, 'they would all, I am sure, have had success in plenty.'

By the end of January sixty-two Allied ships had been sunk– a total of 327,000 tons. Most of this was in American waters and therefore during the second two weeks of the month. As news of the successes, and the continuing potential for good sport, came back to the U-Boat bases, more U-Boats set out with revived enthusiasm burning among their crews. It was discovered, somewhat to the surprise of the U-Boat arm, that medium sized U-Boats could cross the Atlantic, and still have enough fuel there for several weeks of active operations. It was found that on a steady cruise, freed from the need to travel at high speeds, they could conserve fuel to greater extent than was dreamed possible. Engineers helped by devising variations on the mode of travel. They found that travelling submerged on the batteries, for example, proved economical on fuel and allowed almost as much headway as battling against a westerly winter gale on the surface. The crews themselves helped to prolong an operation by sacrificing much of their water supplies and cutting down their drinking and washing in order to carry fuel in the water tanks. And to take full advantage of the extra time which these methods afforded, they gave up most of their already diminutive living space to pack in crates of food and supplies. It was an indication of the eagerness with which the U-Boat crews, many of them newly trained and on their first operation, entered upon this new phase.

Naturally, Doenitz ordered all the U-Boats that were becoming available to be equipped in the ports in western France and to proceed to the American coast as quickly as was compatible with maximum fuel economy. Then on January 22nd he received an order which undercut the strength of his forces considerably. Hitler, it seemed, had had one of his 'intuitions'. He was certain that the Allies were on the point of attempting an invasion of Norway, which he was convinced was the 'zone of destiny'. All available U-Boats were to gather immediately in the waters between Iceland, the Faeroes, and Scotland, to disrupt the anticipated invasion. But apparently this intuition was less strong than some, for on January 23rd Doenitz received a message which completely contradicted the Norway order. The Fuehrer, it seemed, was extremely satisfied with the number of sinkings being recorded off the United States, and he ordered that

Top left Climax to a night attack; a broken vessel goes down in flames. *Top right* Lt-Cdr Zapp, home from American waters and pleased with his success. *Right* In a daylight attack, the gun is used to finish off a torpedoed ship

Time to relax on manoeuvres and watch another ship at work. *Top right* Home at last, captain and crew toast a safe return. *Bottom right* Back from a fruitful voyage, the crew parade on deck under their flag

the U-Boats engaged on that campaign should continue to operate there. The confusion was somewhat clarified on February 6th by a specific order for twelve U-Boats to go to the region of Norway or be kept at readiness in the Norwegian ports, and eight others to be kept in the area of Iceland and the Hebrides. A further order for the transfer of twenty boats to the Norwegian area by February 15th put an end for the time being to Doenitz's plan to reinforce the campaign in the Atlantic.

Since he was left with only about twelve boats to operate at any one time off the coast of America, their success was all the more astonishing. The first group of five U-Boats which opened operation 'Paukenschlag' was followed in mid-January by a further group of five large U-Boats deployed for action in the Caribbean. The date for the launching of their onslaught, carefully fixed to coincide with the new moon and therefore maximum darkness, was February 16th. They had orders direct from Admiral Raeder to attempt not only the sinking of ships, but also the bombardment of the fuel tanks at Aruba and Curaçao, which stood close to the shore. The sinkings began immediately, and Lt-Cdr Hartenstein in U-156 torpedoed two tankers off Aruba. He then decided to try his hand at the bombardment (Doenitz had never had any confidence in the idea) but his first round stuck in the muzzle and exploded. Two ratings were injured and the muzzle was wrecked, but Hartenstein managed to salvage the gun by sawing off the damaged part. He opened fire again, but the coastal defence had recovered from their initial surprise and retaliated, forcing him to break off the engagement. Raeder, anxious to inflict the greatest possible damage on Allied fuel supplies, ordered the bombardment to be resumed the following night, but the defences were too wary to be caught twice, and all shore lights were extinguished. The submarines found it impossible to locate their targets and the idea was dropped.

They returned to their well proven method of operating, and successes began to accumulate. Lt-Cdr Achilles took U-161 right into the harbours at Port of Spain, Trinidad, and Port Castries, Santa Lucia, and sank several ships at anchor. Lt-Cdr Bauer arrived in the Caribbean in a sixth U-Boat at the beginning of March, and within two weeks had achieved a personal tally of nine ships sunk. In U-504 Captain Poske travelled north as far as Florida and was operating off the resorts of Miami and Palm Beach. On February 21st he sank a tanker. The next night he sank a four-masted ship, then another tanker, then yet another tanker in a submerged daylight attack. Then three days later, having evaded a destroyer which located him, he blew up a cargo ship with a load of motor cars on deck.

Apart from minor diversions against the Freetown convoys off the coast of Africa – an attempt to dissuade the Allies from concentrating too much of their anti-submarine effort in the western Atlantic – Doenitz continued to send all the U-Boats he could to American waters. This amounted to no great number, since the German high command had none of Doenitz's singlemindedness about the value of a concerted campaign against merchant shipping. At no time were there more than eight U-Boats at work in this theatre, which for the Allies proved most fortunate, in view of the riot which this handful were running. March and April were the most successful months of all, and in daring individual attacks, mainly against ships sailing alone, a new generation of U-Boat 'aces' came into being, similar to the one which had grown up in attacks on the northern convoy routes before the development of wolf-pack tactics. Operating by night in water often no more than five fathoms deep, which meant they were sitting ducks should a destroyer discover them, they attacked shipping close to the shore. Lt-Cdr Hardegen in U-123 sank eleven ships between mid-march and late April. Lt-Cdr Mohr, in U-124, sank nine, and Lt-Cdrs Lassen in U-160, Muzelburg in U-203, and Topp in U-552 sank at least five each.

Small wonder that the U-Boat commanders referred to the early months of 1942 as their second 'happy time'. The period has also been described as a 'merry massacre' and 'the American shooting season'. All the names are appropriate. The main factor which stopped the U-Boats achieving even greater destruction, apart from their sheer lack of numbers, was their shortage of fuel, which despite the willingness of the crews to go without water, severely abbreviated their working time. To solve this problem Doenitz had under construction a number of U-tankers – large U-Boats of 1,600 tons, insufficiently manoeuvrable for active operations, and in fact equipped only with deck guns for their own protection, and no torpedo tubes. But they carried 700 tons of fuel, and could feed up to 600 tons of it to smaller operational U-Boats. If each of twelve such boats received an' extra fifty tons, their range could be extended to the furthest parts of the Caribbean, or alternatively they could operate for a longer period. But these 'milch cows' as they were inevitably known in the U-Boat arm, were slow in coming forward. The first one, U-459, came into service in April and on the 22nd of that month carried out its first refuelling operation for U-108 under Lt-Cdr Scholtz.

But by this time, American anti-submarine techniques were improving, much to the relief of the British, who noted bitterly that many of their own merchantmen were being lost after they had been successfully escorted across the Atlantic to the American eastern seaboard and delivered to the ill-organised care of the American escort forces. On April 14th the United States destroyer *Roper* notched up its country's first success when it sank U-85, and before long the U-Boats were being forced out of the shallow waters where their pickings were so easy. In the northern part of the American coast at least, the convoy system was beginning to be introduced, and the U-Boats, until then able to roam at random and still be sure of encountering ample targets, suddenly found the coastal waters empty of shipping for long periods at a time. The only successes in early May were achieved off the coast of Florida, where despite improving sea and air patrols, three U-Boats between them sank ten ships.

Further to the south, in the Caribbean, the hey day of the U-Boats was prolonged into May by the failure of the defence forces to apply themselves seriously to the matter of forming convoys and working up anti-submarine measures. It seems that they had not expected U-Boats to operate so far from the Biscay bases. They had reckoned clearly without the advent of the 'milch cows'. These by the middle of June had replenished twenty U-Boats with fuel, which were consequently able to continue operations during the critical weeks before defences were tightened. Six U-Boats, transferred from the North American coast to the Caribbean, and four diverted there while on the way to the then unprofitable eastern seaboard, brought the total of U-Boats which had worked there to thirty-seven. In May and June alone they had sunk no less than 148 ships with a total tonnage of 752,000 tons. Then inevitably, at the beginning of July, these depredations alerted the controllers of shipping in the Caribbean to the advantages of the convoy system, and the Convoy and Routing Section of the United States Fleet set up a complicated network of convoys between Port of Spain in the south, through Aruba, Panama and Key West, and as far as Halifax, Nova Scotia in the north.

To Doenitz it was soon apparent that the pattern was repeating itself. Just as after the first 'happy time' the enemy had taken the protective measure of sailing his ships in convoy, and the U-Boat arm had replied by curtailing the spectacular exploits of lone wolves and forming well-organised and carefully controlled packs, so now individual glory would have to be subordinated to corporate efficiency. Doenitz had foreseen this likelihood in respect of north American coastal waters as early as May. He also saw that, as had happened before, the concentration of defence in the areas of greatest U-Boat activity was

accompanied by a slackening of defensive measures in other areas, which could be used to advantage. Doenitz calculated that since the Atlantic Ocean had been free of U-Boat activity for some time, the convoys would now in all probability be sailing by the most direct route between Newfoundland and Britain (the great circle route). He decided, while the American campaign was still on, to test this theory by forming a wolf pack of eight U-Boats straddled across this line to intercept any convoys using it. He was right, of course. Lt Hinsch in U-569 immediately sighted a convoy steaming more or less on this line, and together with four other U-Boats in the immediate vicinity, he pounced. That first night they destroyed seven ships, and only extremely bad weather, in which contact was lost, allowed the other merchantmen to escape. Several other sightings during the next few days confirmed Doenitz's contention, and from one convoy the corvette *Mimosa* and four other vessels were sunk. These were diversions from the main brunt of the attack during the present phase, but they were a clear promise that when the 'happy time' eventually came to an end, a return to the campaign against the convoys would produce equally worthwhile results.

While it lasted, the American effort had proved more than satisfactory. Of the U-Boats' total sinkings in the first six months of 1942, 585 Allied ships of 3,001,000 tons, by far the great majority was in the western Atlantic and the Caribbean. But even to this bright picture there was a darker side. German Naval statisticians had calculated that victory in the Battle of the Atlantic, based on the premise that shipping must be sunk at a faster rate than the Allies' building programme could replace it, would necessitate the destruction of at least 700,000 tons per month. It was a source of some concern to Doenitz that even with the free run of the American waters, and their paltry defence, the campaign had failed to achieve the specified results. The one mitigating feature at the time was that all the sinkings had been achieved with the loss of only twenty-one U-Boats, only six of them off the American coast. At the beginning of the year, the U-Boat arm had ninety-one operational boats; by the beginning of March the yards were building at an increasing rate, and the operational total had gone up to 111. By the end of June 140 were in operation, and still more were coming forward. The Allies were at this time simply not sinking enough U-Boats to prevent their strength growing, and if the increase were maintained, there was still a possibility of achieving the requisite quantity of ships sunk. After two and a half years of war, the outcome of the struggle for sea supremacy still hung evenly in the balance.

The Arctic Waters: Winter and spring 1942

Crew of a German surface ship sight a
U-Boat through the Arctic mists

In September of 1941 the first of a series of convoys carrying war material from the British Isles to Russia had begun, and the U-Boats stationed in Norway started their long and intense war against this shipping. Conditions for both sides were as difficult and dangerous as any encountered anywhere during the war, with constant storms, freezing temperatures, the ever present danger of pack ice in the Arctic circle, and the difficulty of eternal daylight in summer and eternal darkness in winter. The convoys took up to three weeks to complete the journey to Murmansk or Archangel, and the length of the voyage through those hostile and forbidding waters could be anything up to 2,000 miles, depending on the limits of the pack ice.

The early convoys enjoyed the protection of long dark nights during the winter of 1941-42, but when spring came and longer hours of daylight provided the U-Boats with more opportunities, the Northern Waters flotilla, with a polar bear as their appropriate crest, were able to come into their own.

On March 20th the convoy PQ13 sailed from Reykjavik for Russia, and a day later its opposite number QP9 left Britain for Murmansk. The need for a fuel tanker to accompany the freighters on this long voyage had persuaded the Allies to sail the convoys in 'crossover pairs', so that the tanker could refuel the convoy bound for Russia at the half-way point and then return with the ships making for Britain. For these two the German High Command organised a bigger air and U-Boat offensive than had previously operated. But the proposed attack was not a success. U-655 was the only U-Boat which encountered the ships of QP9, and she was rammed and sunk by the escorting minesweeper *Sharpshooter*. They fared slightly better against the outward bound convoy. On March 29th, after a violent storm had scattered its ships across 150 miles of the arctic seas, U-585, searching for targets over this vast distance, was herself found and sunk by the escort vessel *Fury*. But on the following day the U-Boats got their revenge by sinking two merchantmen from the remnants of the convoy, to add to three sunk by aircraft. For in these northern waters, in contrast to the Atlantic, the battle against the convoys was by no means the exclusive preserve of the U-Boats, and they found themselves playing only an equal part in it alongside surface ships and aircraft. The total which the three services accumulated from PQ13, five ships from the twenty that set sail, was claimed by the Germans as a notable success. The British, while they did not consider the loss a tragedy in itself, were filled with forbodings for the future, and early in April the

In these conditions, efficient operation of a U-Boat was almost impossible

U-Boat in a turbulent sea.

First Sea Lord pointed out to his defence committee that losses might become so great as to make it impossible to continue these convoys.

The victims from the next pair, PQ14 and QP10, five ships from the twenty-four which attempted the two voyages, lent weight to the British opinion. And from the next west bound convoy QP11, U-456 achieved a notable success when she torpedoed and damaged the cruiser *Edinburgh*. German destroyers followed up the attack, and the *Edinburgh's* plight became so bad that her crew had to be taken off by accompanying minesweepers and the British themselves sank her.

By the time convoy PQ16 sailed, it was obvious to the Allies that the U-Boats, surface vessels, and aircraft together were gaining the upper hand in these waters, and the Admiralty strongly recommended that so long as the airfields in northern Norway were open and could be used by German aircraft, the sailing of convoys should be stopped. But the political

argument for maintaining the flow of war material to Russia was overwhelming, and in the full anticipation that disaster, sooner or later, was bound to befall one convoy, it was decided that they would go on.

On May 21st the thirty-five ships of convoy PQ16, and the fifteen ships of QP12 in the other direction, set sail. But it was on neither of these that the expected axe fell. U-Boats sank one ship from the Russia bound convoy on May 26th, but after that they were driven off. Even Doenitz accorded praise to the escorts for that effort, and admitted that the U-Boats had let him down. But their colleagues in the air, while they reported great achievements, in fact fared little better. They delivered a concerted onslaught on PQ16, in which no less than 108 aircraft took part during the day of May 27th alone, but they only managed to sink six more ships. The opposite convoy QP12 arrived without loss.

When PQ17 sailed, at the end of the month, with thirty-six ships, it was only

after considerable misgivings on the part of high ranking officers of the British Admiralty had been supressed, and only with a strong escort of six destroyers, four corvettes, two submarines, two anti-aircraft ships, and three rescue ships. A preliminary brush with the U-Boats on July 1st ended with no damage to either side, but on July 4th the battle was joined in earnest, and three ships were sunk by torpedo aircraft, and one other was damaged. That night, because of the threat of surface action by the German battleships *Tirpitz* and *Scheer*, and the cruiser *Hipper*, the convoy was ordered to scatter. That order, the result of something of a panic on the part of the British, was to have disastrous consequences for them, for in three days the U-Boats and aircraft, running amuck among the widely dispersed and therefore poorly escorted ships, sank seventeen. By the time the shaken remains of the convoy arrived at their destinations and the complete tally could be calculated, the U-Boats had sent ten ships to the bottom, and the aircraft another thirteen merchantmen and one rescue ship. Two of the original thirty-six starters had had the good fortune to turn back during the early stages of the voyage, and of the remainder only eleven merchantmen and two rescue ships survived.

The U-Boats and aircraft had good cause to be pleased with their work. They had prevented the passage to Russia of 210 from 297 aircraft, 430 from 594 tanks, and 3,350 from 4,246 other vehicles. And in addition nearly two thirds of the rest of the cargoes was sunk.

Even if their opportunities for action were few and far between, and even if they suffered the wickedest and most punishing of climatic conditions imaginable, and even if they had to share their achievements with other services, the impact of the U-Boats, when it reached pinnacles such as that, was considerable.

Technical advances: Summer 1942

While the fighting at sea went on with undiminished fury, another less spectacular but no less intensive battle was being fought out behind the scenes – the battle for technical supremacy. The men responsible enjoyed none of the immediate glory that came with success in the fighting, nor suffered the perpetual peril that coloured life at sea, but their influence on the course of the war was none-the-less of paramount importance. Normally, there was nothing sudden about their contribution to the war. Research and development went on unceasingly, and as an important development came to light, it was introduced in small numbers immediately, and more extensively as production increased. Thus the influence of any single technical step was felt over a period, often of several months.

From the early days of 1942, a number of U-Boats, particularly in the Bay of Biscay, reported being attacked on the surface by day. Lookouts in the conning towers were as alert as ever, but they were nevertheless sighting the attacking aircraft long after it had obviously sighted them. More important evidence lay in the practice the aircraft developed of invariably mounting attacks out of the sunlight or out of heavy cloud, which led the Germans to believe that British pilots had sighted the U-Boats at great distances, and had ample time to manoeuvre into a favourable position for

an attack. U-Boat commanders became even more worried when they found themselves, cruising on the surface on extremely dark nights, suddenly picked out with terrifying accuracy in the beam of an aircraft's searchlight. Using this light from a range of up to 2,000 yards, the aircraft homed in and straight away carried out a bombing raid. On June 17th Lt-Cdr Mohr reported that seven times during the course of an attack on convoy ONS100, destroyers had appeared over the horizon bearing down directly on him at great speed; surface vessels had also developed an uncanny new knack.

To Doenitz, it appeared that the British had developed a new and highly efficient long distance surface location device, and he took this mysterious problem to the technical branch of Naval High Command. Their opinion did little to alleviate his difficulty. They believed that the only radar sets in existence were incapable of detecting a submarine on the surface in anything but the calmest water, and then only at the shortest range. What was not known at this stage was that the British had invented a one and a half metre radar set, small enough to be carried in an aircraft, which could well cope with these tasks. Its only disadvantage was its failure to function at close range. In the last stages of an approach the contact faded, and only a visual sighting could pin-point

U-Boat kill: six minutes after attack by
a British Sunderland, the U-Boat sinks by
the stern under a final burst of fire.
Some survivors have escaped into the
water

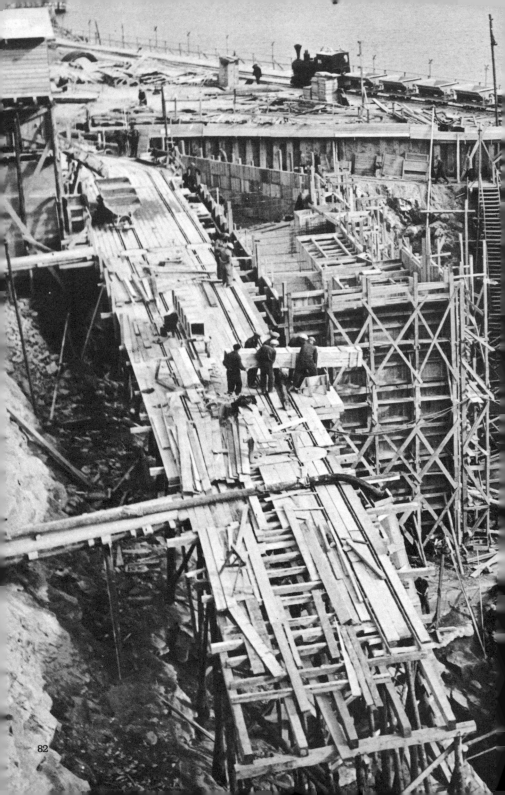

the U-Boat. The British remedied this situation quite early in the war, when Squadron Leader H de V Leigh invented a searchlight suitable for transporting in aircraft. It was obviously some time before it could be fitted extensively into the convoy escorts, but by mid-1942 it was this Leigh Light, used in conjunction with the new radar, which caught the U-Boat commanders so badly off guard. In attacks of this kind, U-502 was lost as it returned from a successful patrol in American coastal waters, U-165 was sunk as it returned to France from Kiel, and three others, U-578, U-705, and U-751, were all put out of action in the Bay of Biscay as they set off for operations, and forced to return to base on the surface.

Doenitz came to the conclusion that nothing other than effective airborne radar could have led to these expensive surprise attacks. He called a meeting in Paris with his technical experts, and after extended discussion they worked out the basis of a plan to combat the radar menace. U-Boats were at once to be equipped with search receivers; with these, they could pick up the signal from an enemy radar set long before they came into the range where the signal was strong enough to be reflected back to the aircraft. The device needed was already available in the French *Metox* set, and aerials were hastily improvised – a length of wire wrapped round a plain wooden frame known colloquially as a 'Biscay Cross'. In addition, immediate steps were ordered to develop and supply the U-Boat with a radar set of their own, which would eliminate the disadvantage of the radar search receiver by giving a clear indication of the aircraft's range and direction. As a further measure, investigations were set in motion to see whether U-Boats could be insulated somehow to prevent the radar signal being sent back to the transmitting aircraft in the form of an echo.

The most urgent step, the search receiver, with its 'Biscay Cross', came into use in the first U-Boat during August. Its effect was immediate, and by October the Allied air offensive against U-Boats leaving and returning to the Biscay ports had ground to a halt. It was something of a stalemate, since as soon as a radar operating aircraft was detected on the receiver, the cross was dismantled and taken below, and the U-Boat dived, which put it out of operation.

The British, in late summer 1942, had available an even better type of radar with a ten centimetre wavelength which they felt would pick up smaller objects at a far greater range, and destroy the advantage gained by the Germans. Fortunately for the U-Boats, the British were handicapped by a lack of inter-unit co-operation more usually found among the German forces. British Bomber Command, desperate for

success in their bomb attacks on Germany, were reluctant to part with any of the new sets, on which they had priority, to Coastal Command. Only the intervention of the Air Ministry solved the problem, when they ordered the diversion of forty sets for fitting into Coastal Command's Wellingtons. This proved little help, however, towards a permanent solution, since those early sets were not specifically designed for anti-submarine work, and it was not until January of 1943 that Coastal Command could be equipped in any significant numbers with its ideal weapon, a radar-fitted bomber from the United States.

In the meantime, U-Boat command set about cementing its temporary advantage over the British aircraft. Doenitz had asked for air cover to escort his damaged U-Boats in the Bay of Biscay back to base, and had received one Focke-Wulf 200, the sum total until then allotted to Atlantic Air Command by Luftwaffe headquarters. Doenitz flew at the beginning of July to Rominten in East Prussia, where he personally requested Goering to supply the planes he needed. Their previous meeting had been hostile, and Doenitz had no great respect for the Reichsmarschall. But he swallowed his aversion, delivered his carefully argued request, and in the end succeeded in extracting from Goering's chief of staff the transfer to his charge of twenty-four JU88C6 heavy fighters. Compared with the usual response to his requests, it was a notable achievement.

As a further defensive measure, all the U-Boats as they returned to base were equipped with four 8 mm machine guns, pending the fitting of more permanent and heavier anti-aircraft weapons, and they were all ordered to travel under water during both day and night except when forced to surface to charge their batteries.

In offensive terms, too, there were developments. Two new torpedo types introduced during late 1942 improved the power of the U-Boats to sink ships once a convoy had been sighted. Both FAT (Flachenabsuchender) and LUT (Lagenuabhängiger) torpedoes could be aimed at a convoy from a distance, and would then run in loops in and out of the lines of ships, with a good chance of hitting one before they ran out of power.

But the key to the future of the U-Boats' war on Allied shipping lay in something far more fundamental than these palliatives. If the British had indeed, as was suspected, produced a radar which could detect them at long range, and which would in all likelihood be improved upon, the U-Boats would be virtually useless in any area over which Allied aircraft could fly. It would not even be essential for the aircraft to make an attack. Its mere appearance, and the threat of bombardment or depth charging, was enough to send a U-Boat

Biscay base under attack; Allied bombs
burst on the U-Boat harbour at Lorient

diving for cover. By the time it was safe to re-surface contact with the convoy would almost certainly be lost. With the range of air cover gradually being extended on both sides of the Atlantic (in mid 1942 the Greenland 'air gap' was down to only 600 sea miles) there was a real prospect that large areas of the oceans, and certainly all coastal waters, would become impossible operating grounds for the whole U-Boat arm.

The changes likely to be imposed on the German Navy's fighting capabilities if these circumstances became widespread were so appalling to Doenitz that on June 24th 1942 he was inspired to write to the Commander-in-Chief requesting a fundamental re-appraisal of the submarine's place in the war.

'We must once again consider whether the submarine with its present power as an instrument of war, is equal to the heavy

**Keeping production up with losses;
U-Boats being built**

demands that are being made of it, or whether hostile defensive measures have not already materially reduced its striking power, and we must also investigate the possible capabilities of enemy anti-sub-marine measures'.

'A study of this kind therefore appears to me to be particularly appropriate just now, when great U-Boat successes in areas weakly defended might well lead us to over-estimate the value of the submarine and lose sight of the true balance between it, as an instrument of war, and the defensive anti-submarine measures taken by the enemy. Its fighting potentialities and characteristics should, in my opinion, be once again subjected to detailed scrutiny, its weakness and the tactical disadvantages which arise from them should be clearly recognized, and the measures necessary in their eradication should be clearly enunciated'.

Doenitz's early conception of the role of the submarine as a 'diving' vessel was, he knew, coming to an end. But what was to

replace it?

The brilliant German submarine designer, Professor Walter, had, in fact, come up with the answer well before the war, but only in theory. Shortage of money, shortage of time, and shortage of confidence on the part of Naval High Command had prevented Walter's idea getting priority over the building of conventional U-Boats. The Walter U-Boat's departure from orthodox design lay in its fundamental capacity to operate in its proper and natural element – *under* water. Instead of having diving equipment and a slow electric motor on which it could skulk about below the waves hoping to creep and squirm away from an attacking destroyer, Walter's boat would operate permanently under water, except when required to come to the surface for the comfort of the crew. Instead of the electric motor, its main underwater propulsion was an engine taking its supply of oxygen from fuel in the form of high strength hydrogen peroxide. A medium sized Walter U-Boat could achieve an underwater speed of 24 knots, and maintain it for six hours. The possibilities which this design offered were enormous. No longer would the submarine commander have to disappear over the horizon to spend hours or even days working his way ahead of a sighted convoy into a good attacking position. He could sail into the attack at will. A U-Boat operating at those speeds could lure away destroyers from the convoy, let in others in a pack, and even race the escort back to the target. Generally, they would be able to tease and toy with the target. Most important, a submerged U-Boat would have nothing to fear from the airborne radar which presented the gravest threat to their immediate operations. Doenitz explained his confidence in the Walter boat in his letter of June 24th to High Command. The letter ended: 'The immediate development, testing, and most rapid construction of the Walter U-Boat is, in my opinion, an essential measure and one which will decide the whole issue of the war'.

Return to the convoy routes

Escorting a convoy, the bridge officers of a British destroyer scan the surface for any sign of a U-Boat

As the introduction of the convoy system brought to an end the extraordinarily successful period off the coast of America and in the Caribbean, the battle swung back again to the convoy routes in the North Atlantic. Doenitz could well see that the increased protection for the newly formed American coastal convoys, and for the Arctic convoys of war materials to Russia, was making demands on the limited escorts available with a consequent reduction in the protection for the shipping in the Atlantic. His selective attacks of the summer had proved his theories to be correct. What he did not know at that time was that the escorts were also reduced by the demands made by preparations for the Allied landings which were to come late in 1942 in North Africa. Ultimately, this was to have great significance, but not during the present phase.

Nor was the deficiency of escorts the only feature which made those convoy routes attractive. They offered Doenitz the chance of keeping far more of his U-Boats on active operations. Long journeys to and from the Caribbean would be cut drastically, allowing each U-Boat to spend a far greater proportion of any sortie on its principal task of sinking shipping, and allowing a greater number of U-Boats to be engaged on that task at any given time. It was here, also, that the convoys were still devoid of the air cover which was proving the best possible counter measure to the U-Boats' attacks. Doenitz knew that he would be wise to take advantage of this situation while it lasted. The 'air gap' which in 1941 had stretched from within 500 miles of the Newfoundland coast to the same distance from the European coast, was now considerably shorter, and likely to contract still further. Four engined aircraft were flying out from bases in North America and Greenland, Iceland and Northern Ireland, and for the convoys off the African coast from Freetown. The field of operations for the U-Boats was consequently quite short, and their only chance of achieving any results lay in making contact with a convoy at one or other extremity of the 'air gap', and pursuing it for several days until it came once more within the range of shorebased aircraft. Fortunately for the U-Boats, the convoys were compelled to adhere to the shortest 'great circle' route across the Atlantic by their severe shortage of fuel, which improved the prospects of a sighting.

On the other hand, the difficulties of the U-Boat arm were aggravated by the comparative inexperience of many of the crews and their commanders. The 'aces' of the early days were for the most part men whose long training in pre-war years had equipped them to carry out their tasks with supreme skill and confidence. Now, as the U-Boat building programme produced increasing numbers of boats – in July 1942 there were 331 in commission – their crews were inevitably recruits fresh from their initial training. Moreover, the need for them to take part in the fight against convoys was so great that they were often directed into an attack immediately after breaking off a previous one. Often in the intervening period they were compelled to fit in, in a short time, the process of re-fuelling from the 'milch cow' at sea, which demanded great navigational skill, and extreme vigilance, in view of the possibility of a chance sighting by enemy escorts while the boats were linked up on the surface. The strain of two or three such operations, one after the other, was too much to expect any crew to undergo, least of all a crew on its first tour of duty, and it proved essential to bring them back to base regularly for a good rest.

In view of these problems, on July 27th Doenitz took the step of instilling a sense of reality in Germany by broadcasting a warning of the difficult times that lay ahead. The German people were cock-ahoop at the U-Boats' achievements, but after the great successes of the previous months – 144 ships of 700,000 tons in June for example – sinkings in July were falling. Doenitz's statement brought the public swiftly down to earth with a forecast of heavy losses. The British Admiralty, pre-dictably, took this as an indication that Doenitz was planning to consolidate his return to the Atlantic convoy routes. They called it a 'tip from the horse's mouth'. And they were right.

Two convoy attacks by a pack of U-Boats during the last weeks of July failed, largely as a result of weather conditions, a cyclone having protected the first and fog the second. Then Lt-Cdr Kelbling in U-593 made contact with another convoy, SC94, sailing east from Nova Scotia. He kept contact for several days, until eventually, on August 5th, the other boats in his group joined him. The escort consisted of a destroyer and six corvettes. Early on, the destroyer was detached from the convoy to guide back to it a number of ships which had become dispersed in dense fog. It was during the destroyer's absence that the U-Boats torpedoed and sank their first ship, *Spar*. The swirling fog helped to protect the U-Boats, but on the afternoon of August 6th it suddenly cleared for an instant, and Lt-Cdr Lemcke, in U-210, found himself on the surface in clear view from the convoy. The destroyer, *Assiniboine*, and the corvette, *Dianthus*, swung towards him and forced him to dive. Down came the depth charges, and U-210 was badly dam-aged. After an apparent eternity the depth charging stopped, and the U-Boat, in bad condition, could stay submerged no longer.

Hoping to find that the escorts had broken off the chase, Lempke brought his leaking boat to the surface to try a fast escape under diesel engines. He found he had surfaced five miles from the *Assiniboine*, but he was in for more than his share of bad luck that day. Once again the fog patches cleared, and the destroyer's crew were given a clear sight of the U-Boat. *Assiniboine* once more plunged through the fog after it, losing sight and picking it up again until eventually it came into good gunning range. A shell hit the U-Boat's conning tower, but the U-Boat replied with a shot which started a fire in the destroyer, killed one man, and wounded thirteen others. Lemcke skilfully flung his boat into tight turns to avoid the *Assini-boine's* attempts to ram, and even pulled off the daring manoeuvre of sailing so close to the destroyer as to prevent her guns being brought to bear: tucked under the destroyer's side he was, for a moment, safe. But it was no permanent solution. As another tactic he tried to dive, but the destroyer came round under full helm and at last succeeded in ramming. Then again she caught the U-Boat with a glancing blow, and as she rode on over it, depth charges were dropped from her stern. Finally, a 4.7 inch shell struck the U-Boat in the bows, and after Lemcke and his crew had abandoned ship, she sank. The survivors were rescued by *Assiniboine* and the corvette *Dianthus*, which came up just in time to witness the end of the duel, but they had the satisfaction of knowing that they had so badly damaged the *Assiniboine* that she had to leave the convoy and make straight for base.

During the next three days the five corvettes which now constituted the entire escort were kept busy chasing away four sighted submarines. On the afternoon of August 8th, a fine summer day, the U-Boats struck again. Five ships were hit by torpe-does within minutes. Three sank im-mediately. The explosions on the other two, which stayed afloat for a time, sent panic and confusion racing through the convoy, and the frightened crews of three other vessels stopped engines and took to the boats. The gun crew of one ship simply leaped overboard. Two of the crews woke up at last to the fact that their ships had not been torpedoed, went back on board, and got their charges under way again. But the third crew had left theirs, the *Radchurch*, for good. Drifting helplessly on the ocean, it was soon sunk by a U-Boat. Throughout that afternoon and night the attacks went on. The corvette *Dianthus*, which had been scurrying about the convoy with great energy in search of the U-Boats, finally had her moment of glory when she depth charged Lt-Cdr Kettner's U-379, forced it to surface, and finally rammed and sank it. Other U-Boats were to a large extent kept on the defensive by the escort, and three were damaged, but between them they accounted for four more merchant vessels. Doenitz sent U-Boat reinforcements to the scene on the afternoon of August 9th, and the British replied by reinforcing the escort vessels, but it was the progress of the convoy itself which ultimately brought its salvation, as it sailed into the range of Liberators flying from Northern Ireland. That day the U-Boats could do no more. Although next morning, in the early hours of daylight before the bombers arrived, they sank four more ships, they were forced from then on to stay submerged, and Doenitz called off

the attack. The wolf pack had sunk eleven ships of more than 52,000 tons.

On the more southerly convoy routes the U-Boats were having similar successes. Operating in the Azores 'air gap' where shipping was out of the range of air cover from Gibraltar, but not yet in range of that from the British Isles, they attacked convoy SL118, which sailed on August 14th, and its successor, SL119. From the two, the U-Boats sank five ships of a total of 42,000 tons. Only U-566 under Lt-Cdr Remus was damaged, but her crew were able to repair the wounds and she reached base.

In September the attacks went on, some successful, others not so. The west bound

Handling a torpedo on deck

91

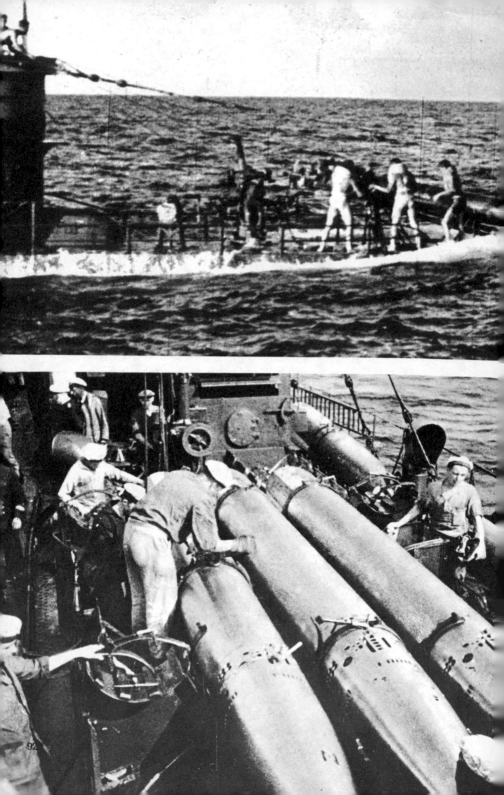

The crew haul the torpedo aboard up a ramp. *Below left* Torpedoes ready for handing over from the torpedo boat to the U-Boat. *Below right* Handling is easier if the U-Boat is slightly submerged

The moment of explosion; a torpedoed
vessel is lost in smoke and spray

convoy ON127 was sighted out in the north Atlantic, beyond the reach of air cover, and the U-Boats kept up a relentless attack for four days. This time they got the better of the escort, which was entirely Canadian and was not equipped with radar. The U-Boats sank seven merchant ships, totalling 50,000 tons, and damaged four others, and also sank the destroyer *Ottawa*, without loss or damage to a single U-Boat.

It was in September that the U-Boat arm was involved in an unfortunate incident which resulted in lengthy and world-wide repercussions. In mid-August a convoy of four U-Boats and a 'milch-cow' had sailed from the Biscay ports to operate against targets just south of the equator. Their orders were to attack only really valuable targets in that region, since too much torpedo activity might tempt the Allies to build up their escorts on the convoy routes from Cape Town before really worthwhile sinkings had been achieved. On September 12th U-156, under Lt-Cdr Hartenstein, sank the British liner *Laconia*, which had on board a British crew, 268 British servicemen and their families going on leave, and 1,800 Italian prisoners of war. When Doenitz learned who the passengers were, he ordered Hartenstein and other U-Boats to pick up survivors. While Hartenstein had his U-Boat full of those rescued, and was towing others in lifeboats to meet a Vichy French warship from Dakar, an American Liberator aircraft flew over him, circled, and dropped bombs. In order to preserve his U-Boat Hartenstein transferred into the lifeboats all the survivors he had on board, cast them off, and submerged to make his escape. Doenitz subsequently sent a signal ordering Hartenstein to take all measures to ensure the safety of his boat, including abandoning rescue operations. Later that night, September 16th, Doenitz ordered his other U-Boats to retain only Italians on board, and transfer all other rescued personnel to the lifeboats. That afternoon U-506, which had not yet done so and still had 142 survivors including women and children on board, was attacked and bombed by a flying boat, but its bombs fortunately exploded when U-506 was 200 feet below the surface. As a result of that attack Doenitz subsequently issued instructions to all U-Boat commanders in what came to be known as the 'Laconia order'. It stipulated that all attempts to rescue the crews of sunken ships would cease, including picking up men from the sea, righting capsized lifeboats, and supplying food and water. Doenitz explained that these activities stood in the way of the main object of the U-Boat war, the destruction of enemy ships and their crews.

The controversy following the 'Laconia order' blew up to international proportions, and it was widely held that it was in fact an order from Doenitz to his U-Boat commanders to murder survivors in the water. After the war ended, the International Military Tribunal at Nuremberg found that this was not so, and cleared Doenitz of that accusation.

The attention currently being paid to the *Laconia* affair and the fate of its survivors did not, of course, prevent the attacks on the convoys continuing. In mid-September, the number of U-Boats on operations in the north Atlantic rose to twenty, but heavy storms blew up, in which neither the escorts nor the merchant ships nor the U-Boats could pay the slightest attention to each other, so urgent was the need to concentrate on their own safety. The violent weather went on into early October, and the ships of both sides, often within sight and gunnery range of each other, could do nothing but try to ride out the gales. Those conditions, while hardly pleasant, brought salvation to a number of convoys.

On October 10th a group of ten U-Boats was cruising off Newfoundland waiting to intercept east-bound convoys from the United States. The twenty U-Boats were divided into two packs, and one was ordered to patrol at the edge of the 'air gap' in the expectation of coming across the convoy SC104 from Sydney, Nova Scotia. All that was in fact sighted was a solitary corvette, at the northern end of the patrol line, and it appeared that their quarry had evaded them. Doenitz immediately turned the whole pack to the north east and sent them racing off to where he imagined the convoy would now be. He was exercising, with virtually no concrete evidence, that sixth sense which both sides, the U-Boat arm and the escort organisation alike, were not only developing but were recognising as a highly relevant instrument in tracking down enemy vessels and predicting their movements. Doenitz's intuition paid off. On October 12th one of the boats again spotted the corvette, and, undetected, followed her right to the convoy. There were forty-seven ships, and an escort of only two destroyers and four corvettes. The air was soon full of messages calling up other U-Boats for the attack, and the signals were of course intercepted. With their high-frequency direction finders to aid them the escorts bore down on the U-Boats, and forced many of them to submerge. But Lt-Cdr Trojer in U-221 penetrated the ranks of the convoy and on that first night sank three ships. Conditions were ideal for U-Boat operations. The small surface escorts were tossed about on the heavy Atlantic swell and could barely operate their asdics, so that once submerged, a U-Boat was virtually safe. The next night Trojer was again in among the ships, and picking his targets with ease sank four more. His personal total from that convoy was seven ships of over 40,000 tons. Between them the remainder of the U-Boats managed to sink only one other ship, and in the attack two U-Boats were lost. U-619 was rammed at high speed by the destroyer *Viscount* on the night of October 15th, and as the continuing improvement in the weather made the task of the escort so much easier the destroyer *Fame* located and depth charged U-353. U-353 came to the surface and its crew hurriedly abandoned ship, but before the U-Boat sank, a boarding party from *Fame* went on board and seized a quantity of the ship's papers which provided valuable intelligence for the Allies.

The pressure of the attacks continued to increase towards the end of October, and as soon as a sighting was reported, or an enemy signal deciphered, the packs of U-Boats were deployed to pursue it, which they did, even in those weeks of unfavourable weather, with unabated enthusiasm. But it was often a merely fortuitous sighting which led a convoy into the path of a patrol of U-Boats. On October 26th, for example, while they were hunting an anticipated west-bound convoy, a patrol line found the east-bound convoy HX212 steering straight for its centre. Those boats in the middle of the line fell back before the approach of the convoy, and the outlying boats converged, drawing the merchant ships innocently into the jaws of their trap. The storms had died down sufficiently for the U-Boats to aim and fire torpedoes, but there was still too much sea to give the escorts a clear radar picture or permit accurate use of the asdic. During the night of October 28th they fell upon their prey and sank seven ships of 52,000 tons.

Two days later one of a group sighted a convoy sailing eastwards hard under the Newfoundland coast, and a lucky wireless interception told U-Boat command the course which this convoy, SC107, would follow. It was easy to set up the remainder of the group for an attack. Fortunately for the U-Boats, the convoy kept to the broadcast route, and six were brought into contact. Unwisely, however, they showed their hand while still within the range of aircraft from Newfoundland, and U-520 and U-658 were sunk by planes of the Royal Canadian Air Force. By November 1st the convoy had passed the limit of the air escort, and in two nights the U-Boats sank fifteen ships of 88,000 tons. Then aircraft flown from Iceland arrived, and a Liberator sank U-132. From that point continuous air cover could be expected, and the attack was therefore called off. To the south, an attack on convoy SL125 off Madeira proved eminently successful. It lasted for seven nights, and in persistent attacks the U-Boats sank thirteen ships of 86,000 tons without loss to themselves.

As it happened, SL125 proved an effective, if expensive, decoy which lured the U-Boats away from even more promising targets. At that time large numbers of troop transports and supply ships were sailing towards Gibraltar for the Allied armies taking part in 'Operation Torch', their campaign in North Africa. In addition to functioning as a decoy, SL125, by suffering a prolonged attack, kept the Allies adequately in the picture regarding the whereabouts of most of the U-Boats in the region, and they were able to divert the troop transports away from trouble.

The landings in North Africa, largely owing to the total failure on the part of the German intelligence service, took German High Command completely by surprise. On November 8th Doenitz received news of American landings on the coast of Morocco, and he immediately diverted all U-Boats operating between Cape Verde Islands and Gibraltar to make immediately for the Moroccan coast. All the U-Boats in the North Atlantic, except those with insufficient fuel to make the journey worthwhile, were also diverted to the Gibraltar area. They began arriving on November 11th, only to find, as anticipated, that the landings were covered by heavy concentrations of destroyers, aircraft, even radar establishments set up on shore. Even so, the U-Boats began their attacks with great bravery. Lt Schweichel in U-173 broke through the protective cordon and scored hits on three ships, none of which sank. During the evening of November 12th, Cdr Kals in U-150 crept along the coast close inshore, using his periscope for the briefest glances, and sank three transports, then with the audacity that wins battles, while the escorts expected their quarry to bolt for the open sea, he crept even closer to the coast and escaped to the north.

Doenitz had grave reservations about the employment of U-Boats off the Straits of Gibraltar. Ample targets were there, certainly, but the strong air and surface escorts so completely inhibited the activities of the U-Boats, and destroyed so many of them before they were able even to begin an action that Doenitz was prompted to describe the area as 'murderous'. His disappointment on receiving, in mid-November, orders to maintain twenty U-Boats constantly operational off the Straits, as well as to replace the large numbers lost in the Mediterranean, was therefore understandable. He promptly submitted his objections to Naval High Command, and was allowed to reduce the twenty to twelve, and send only four boats into the Mediterranean as replacements, regardless of the numbers lost.

What distressed Doenitz most about the order was its arrival at a time when, because of the Allied concentration on the North Africa landings, and the generous protection given to troopships and supply vessels, Atlantic convoys would be virtually devoid of escorts. Doenitz always saw the war against Allied shipping in its broadest outline. Any sinking, of any ship anywhere, he knew, would have its repercussions not only in the area where it occurred but throughout the Allied network of supply and communication. Except in one or two particular circumstances where a lightning strike could disrupt an actual operation, Doenitz regarded it as lunacy to nullify the potential of a U-Boat by working it against the heaviest possible concentrations of escort vessels.

It was with these considerations in mind that Doenitz managed, with permission, slightly to bend the November order, and move his Gibraltar boats out into mid-Atlantic, west of the Azores, to intercept convoys of reinforcements for the American landing forces. But the move was not radical enough to restore success in any significant measure, and only four ships were sunk, on December 6th. By December 23rd Naval High Command had come to the same opinion as Doenitz regarding the futility of operations against the Allied North African landings, and these activities were called off.

Meanwhile the few U-Boats whose fuel supplies had been inadequate to bring them to the Moroccan coast in early November, and the eight for whom Doenitz had secured a reprieve from the Gibraltar patrol, were at work against the normal convoy routes. On November 17th and 18th the first group attacked convoy ONS144 in the 'air gap' and sank five merchant ships plus a corvette from the escort. Then their fuel supplies did run out, and they converged on the submarine tanker U-460 to refuel. It was then that the hurricane broke. For days they were tossed about the ocean without the power to make sufficient way to keep themselves steady. Electric lighting and cooking were halted because the batteries could not be recharged, and when the storm ultimately died down, they all had to use their radios extensively to re-establish contact with the tanker. With no electric power, and no fuel to re-charge their batteries, they were unable to submerge, and could only pray that their signals would not bring the enemy on the scene. But finally they all met the 'milch cow', refuelled and re-stocked, and set course hurriedly for the Biscay bases.

A few moderate successes followed, although they were marred by the accidental sinking of U-254 after a collision with another U-Boat. Then in the middle of December the weather once more blew up with such violence that operations had again to be suspended, and not until December 27th was it possible to attack a convoy. In two nights, taking advantage of the screen of fog which intermittently lifted and fell around the ships, the U-Boats sank thirteen vessels from ONS 154, a total of 67,000 tons. The attack brought to an end the year's actions against the North Atlantic convoy routes.

Throughout the second half of 1942, in parallel with these main attacks, small groups of U-Boats had been making their impact against shipping in more distant waters. The introduction of the convoy system off the American coast had made that region untenable for the U-Boats, but in the waters of the Caribbean and off Trinidad many ships were still sailing independently, and there remained good prospects of surprise attacks. A particularly good area was the Windward Passage between Cuba and Haiti. Here, by August, convoys were operating, but shipping travelling westwards from Trinidad and northwards from Panama was forced by the geography of the islands to converge. The routes taken by merchant ships were so predictable that a U-Boat making a contact could easily direct others on to a likely course. Air escort was active, but the U-Boat captains soon discovered that boldness paid rich dividends, and that their greatest immunity was to be found inside the columns of the convoy, or close to the escort vessels themselves, where airborne radar almost invariably failed to find them. In August 1942 these tactics led to the sinking of fifteen ships of 87,603 tons. Two U-Boats were lost, and then, as the escorts got over their surprise at these tactics, they became more skilful and alert and the U-Boats were forced to withdraw to the waters around Trinidad, to the estuary of the Orinoco river, and to the Guiana coast. Shipping was spasmodic, but when it did appear, heavy, and with only eight U-Boats operating, no less than twenty-nine ships were sunk in September, of a total of 143,000 tons. In contrast to the Windward Passage sinkings, these successes continued into October, with seventeen ships of 82,000 tons, and November with twenty-five ships of 150,000 tons.

The waters off Freetown also provided opportunities for action, though it was by no means the rich vein of gold the U-Boat arm had hoped it would be. And across the other side of the straits between Africa and South America the declaration of war by Brazil gave the opportunity for an extension of operations off that coast, particularly against the formations of valuable refrigerated ships carrying meat for the people of Britain. But by far the most important of the distant waters was the Cape Town region, where no U-Boats had previously operated. When he sent his boats there Doenitz estimated that the element of surprise would almost certainly lead to valuable successes. It was a voyage of 6,000 miles, and could only be contemplated with the aid of a 'milch cow' to replenish fuel and supplies during the journey. The first group, called the 'polar bear' group, composed of Type IXC submarines together with a U-tanker, left their bases in mid-August and after re-fuelling in the South Atlantic reached Cape Town.

But surprise was lost. Somehow, the British Admiralty's submarine tracking room had, it later transpired, got wind of the movement of U-Boats to the south, and all shipping had been hurriedly re-routed away from Cape Town. Instead of shipping routes crowded with victims waiting to be picked off, the U-Boats found a vast and empty sea, and had to forage for their prey. Simultaneously with the arrival of that group of IXC U-Boats, the first commissioned boat of an important new class, Type IXD2, arrived off Cape Town. These were the 'gun cruisers' of pre-war design, but they had been converted so that their main armament was the torpedo. With a displacement of 1,365 tons, they had a range of 31,500 miles, and were particularly suitable for these long range operations. U-179, under Lt-Cdr Sobe, proved its value by sinking a ship in its first attack, but it was then spotted by the destroyer *Active* on that same day and sunk. The Type IXC boats, despite finding no easy targets, turned out to be immensely successful in their search for shipping, and by the end of October had sunk twenty-four vessels of 161,000 tons, including the troopships *Oronsay* of 24,043 tons, *Orcades* of 33,450 tons, and *Duchess of Atholl* of 20,119 tons.

These and other successes were wholly attributable to the lack of escorts for this shipping. Re-routing them was not enough: there were still plenty of targets to keep the U-Boats active, providing they went out and searched for them. The British Admiralty countered by ordering out to Cape Town twelve anti-U-Boat trawlers from the Western Approaches, plus eighteen others which they had lent to the United States Navy Department in the previous February and which were now released, plus destroyer and corvette reinforcements from the Halifax Escort Force and the Eastern Fleet. But it was almost the end of the year before they arrived and could be organised into an efficient escort fleet. Doenitz's decision to expend time and fuel on a long distance project to seek out and attack the enemy in his 'soft spots' was thus fully justified.

During the middle of October the short range U-Boats of the 'polar bear' group were forced by shortage of fuel to return to base, but continuity was maintained by the arrival of the next three long range boats. These, in addition to working the waters of Cape Town in the South Atlantic, moved into the Indian Ocean as far as the Mozambique Channel, and there not only sank twenty-four ships of 127,201 tons, including more troopships, but disrupted shipping so badly that the port of Lourenço Marques had twice to be closed, which had useful repercussions in disrupting supplies of fuel for the Allies in the Middle East.

By December the Allied escorts had started to arrive, and protected convoys were established between Durban and Cape Town. In that month, only five ships of 23,251 tons were sunk, and another lightning strike campaign began to draw to a close. These campaigns were proving of immense worth, not only in supplementing the sinkings of shipping on the main North Atlantic convoy routes but also in distracting escorts from that main theatre to any regions where a temporary onslaught could be mounted. As long as U-Boats command kept one move ahead of the enemy, and withdrew as soon as the escorts began to build up, these 'guerilla' style operations could help to keep the Axis powers on top in their war on Allied shipping.

During the last six months of 1942, sinking by Axis submarines, mostly of course by German U-Boats, was maintained at a tolerably high level, if not up to the average of 700,000 tons which was regarded as essential to bring the Allies to their knees. The figures were: July, ninety-six ships of 476,065 tons; August, one-hundred-and-eight ships of 544,410 tons; September, ninety-eight ships of 485,413 tons; October, ninety-four ships of 619,417 tons; November, one hundred-and-nine ships of 729,160 tons; and December sixty ships of 330,816 tons.

The total losses inflicted on the enemy by Axis submarines during the year amounted to 1,160 ships of 6,266,215 tons, and other arms of the German and other Axis forces pushed this total up to 7,790,697 tons. In that time the Germans had lost only eighty-seven U-Boats, or 8.9 per cent of their numbers at sea, and they now had 212 boats operational out of 393 in service, compared with ninety-one operational out of 249 at the beginning of the year.

The Allies, on the other hand, though the Germans had no accurate knowledge to that effect at the time, had built just over seven million tons of new ships. The year had thus produced a nominal gain to the German cause in the 'tonnage war'.

At the end of 1942 the decisive moves in the struggle for domination of the high seas, on which the whole outcome of the war so clearly depended, had still not arrived.

Climax of the battle: March 1943

At the beginning of 1943, severe weather conditions brought an almost total stoppage in the front line of the battle at sea, as the storms which had whipped the North Atlantic during the preceding months mounted to unprecedented fury. Operating the tiny U-Boat on the pitching and heaving seas was a task filled with hazard and danger. Apart from having to stay lashed to the boat when on the bridge, U-Boat crews found it virtually impossible to keep an accurate track of their own position. Stars and sun were hidden by thick cloud, and celestial navigation was therefore out of the question. And with the constant twisting and turning, at slow speeds and fast, involved in any U-Boat sortie dead-reckoning was a most unreliable means of finding a U-Boat's whereabouts. During the first two weeks of January, not surprisingly, not a convoy was sighted, even with 164 operational boats to scour the Atlantic.

While the boats at sea spent their days and nights battling with the elements and bent on self-preservation, events of considerable importance took place behind the scenes on both sides.

At the Casablanca Conference which began on January 14th the Allies decided that in view of the losses to merchant shipping, and the failure to meet and beat the numbers lost by building replacements, it was essential that the U-Boats should be defeated in the Battle of the Atlantic. The Allies clearly realised what a paramount menace the U-Boats were to their cause – an outlook which Doenitz had long and vainly tried to impress on his superiors. The Allies saw that their plan to invade Europe could never be brought to fruition until the ocean through which their supplies were constantly channelled were rid once and for all of the scourge of the U-Boat. Victory in this battle was therefore raised to top priority, and all Allied resources were to be directed to its end. If only Doenitz had been blessed with a High Command which held the same appreciation of the significance of the U-Boat! Fortunately for the Germans, the Allies reduced the effect of this fundamentally sound outlook when they decided to implement it by dropping bombs on the U-Boat bases in the Bay of Biscay. It was understood that no bombs could possibly damage the U-Boat shelters to the extent required, and the policy of area bombing to destroy the installations and towns round the bases was put into effect. On the night of January 14th 101 aircraft attacked the port of Lorient, and on January 15th this was followed by a second attack of 131 bombers. When daylight came the Americans felt that they could improve on the performance and they had a shot at precision bombing of the submarine pens themselves. Heavy raids followed on the port of

Grand Admiral Raeder and the Fuehrer; picture taken in January 1943 at the time of Raeder's resignation

St Nazaire. Despite two written protests in late January from the Commander-in-Chief of RAF Bomber Command that his own raids were doing nothing to assist in the prosecution of the war against the U-Boats, the attacks went on with intensity until mid-summer of that year, and sporadically until the end of the war.

The bombardment was a gigantic waste of effort. The area bombing did nothing to disrupt the building programme to any significant extent, and the precision bombing damaged no U-Boat, nor even penetrated a single shelter.

On the German side, January brought a major upheaval in the naval hierarchy. Relations between Raeder and Hitler had never been particularly cordial, and on January 6th when the two met in conference Hitler flew into a flaming rage over the way the battleship *Lutzow* and the cruiser *Hipper* had performed in an unsuccessful attack on a British convoy on the last day of 1942. Raeder was given little opportunity to speak, but instead was subjected to an uninhibited verbal assault for ninety minutes, and dismissed with instructions to draw up plans to pay off all the big ships in the German Navy. Over a week later Raeder submitted a paper in which he attempted to dissuade the Fuehrer from his decision. But Hitler remained adamant. Raeder resigned on January 30th, and Hitler appointed Doenitz to the post of Commander-in-Chief in his place. The most important aspect of this promotion was that Doenitz proved far too astute to take the obvious advantage of it. Rather than allow himself to be drawn away from the main centre of the battle and elevated into the abstract realms of policy making, he remained Flag Officer, U-Boats. From this dual position he knew he could both push the interests of the U-Boat arm, which he still believed to be the key factor in the outcome of the war, and also retain a firm hold on the detailed running of the cam-

paign. Day to day decisions were left to Rear-Admiral Godt, Doenitz's Chief of Staff, but Doenitz himself, knowing that no other officer had his knowledge or experience in U-Boats, continued to be responsible for the way U-Boats were used. It was a strong position to be in. Later he also got away with scrapping the idea to decommission the big ships.

While the weather on the North Atlantic convoy routes prevented any active operations, further to the south, where the January climate held nothing like the same ferocity, the 'Delphin' group was carrying out westward sweeps along the great circle route from Morocco to New York, hoping to intercept convoys bringing supplies and reinforcements to the troops who had landed in North Africa. But it was the solitary U-514, cruising off Trinidad, which opened the new year's activities, when on January 3rd it sighted a group of north-bound tankers sailing almost certainly to Gibraltar with fuel for those troops. The U-Boat, unhappily, lost contact. It was then that Doenitz took one of his boldest decisions. Against all the protestations of his junior officers, who wanted the 'Delphin' group to attack another convoy recently sighted, he ordered the eight U-Boats in this patrol to form up into a line and try to intercept the tanker convoy. The distance between them was a thousand miles, their chance of an interception slim. But the prize was enormous; stopping a convoy carrying fuel, in view of its effects on the work of soldiers on the ground, was one of the greatest opportunities a U-Boat group could possibly hope for. For several days they cruised back and forth in their search, until at dawn on January 8th Doenitz's boldness was rewarded. The convoy ran right into the middle of their formation. The U-Boat commanders knew they had been presented with a gift, and they did not turn it down. In attacks which went on until

Torpedo strike on an enemy ship

January 11th the U-Boats sank seven of the nine tankers in the convoy, without loss to themselves. It was a brilliant operation, in its conception, execution, and effect. Well knowing what the loss of this fuel meant to the Allied armies in Africa, the German Commander-in-Chief there, General von Arnim, telegrammed his thanks to Doenitz.

The first sinking on the North Atlantic convoy routes came at the end of January when the weather at last improved. The fast convoy HX224 was attacked and three ships eliminated from it. Among the survivors picked up was a British officer who told his captors of another convoy sailing in the wake of HX224, some two days behind. It was intelligence of immense value. A concentration of twenty U-Boats was brought into line and the prisoner's information proved accurate. The convoy steamed straight for them. With sixty-three ships carrying valuable war material, the escort was particularly strong, and included no less than twelve warships. Consequently the battle was fierce, and three-quarters of the U-Boats suffered depth charge attacks at some stage in the fighting. Three U-Boats were sunk, and two others damaged, but the pack accounted for thirteen ships of nearly 60,000 tons.

In that encounter, it was largely the lack of training on the part of the convoy's escorts that finally swung the balance in favour of the U-Boats. By contrast, the virtue of experience and training was clearly evident when the next convoy was sighted on February 17th. Among its escort were the two old enemies of the U-Boats, *Fame* and *Viscount*, which had sunk two U-Boats when convoy SC104 was attacked in the previous October. Because of extremely bad conditions only two U-Boats could be brought into the attack. *Fame* sank U-201, *Viscount* sank U-69.

As the weather improved, and the numbers of U-Boats at sea increased, the rate of sinking began to rise again. On February 21st the convoy ON166 was attacked and in four days of fighting fourteen ships of 85,000 tons were sunk. Then ON167 was located and attacked. In the Trinidad waters Mohr by himself sank four ships of 23,566 tons from one convoy. On February 27th the fast convoy HX227 was attacked and two ships of 14,352 tons were sunk. Then SC121 was located, lost, and located again, and the U-Boats destroyed thirteen of its ships, a total of 62,198 tons. These and other achievements raised the indifferent January total of thirty-nine ships of 203,128 tons, to a more respectable tally in February of sixty-three ships of 359,328 tons.

These results were to a large extent directly attributable to the work of the Naval High Command's cryptographic section – 'B' Service. They were busy throughout U-Boat operations intercepting and deciphering the Allies' signals to

convoys, and they achieved remarkable and repeated successes. The British, of course, were busy at the same time intercepting and deciphering messages between U-Boats and headquarters. These activities often cancelled each other out. The Allies, having worked out the likely dispositions of the U-Boats, proceeded to re-route their convoys accordingly. Interception by 'B' Service of these Allied signals would lead the U-Boats back into the path of the re-directed shipping. The Allies then, of course, often managed to intercept the signals to U-Boats, and changed their convoy routes yet again. The two sides expended a great deal of energy and concentrated some of their best brains in this complex but vital intelligence game.

An example of how it might be played occurred on March 9th when 'B' Service gave the location of the fast convoy HX228 sailing directly for a group of U-Boats but still several hundred miles away from it. Attempting to out-think the enemy, U-Boat command put themselves in his place – a regular and often fruitful exercise. They assumed that the Allies would by now know where the U-Boats were, and would re-direct the convoy to the north. They therefore replied by re-directing the U-Boats to the north. As it happened, the convoy was not re-directed, and it sailed past them to the south.

Did the U-Boats out-think themselves? Did the Allies in fact not know of the existence of that U-Boat group? Or did they pick up the signals ordering the U-Boats to the north and so maintain course? Or did they, perhaps, thinking one move further ahead, anticipate that Doenitz would expect the convoy to be re-routed and would send his U-Boats north, and therefore stay on course? The details of that battle of wits will never be known. In the end, at any rate, some of the U-Boats turned about, caught up with the convoy, and redeemed themselves by sinking four ships and the destroyer *Harvester*, although U-432 and U-444 were lost.

'B' Service also played an important part in guiding the U-Boats into the way of two convoys against which their operations produced possibly the best results of the war. The cryptographic section, having recently broken the code then in use, deciphered a message and informed U-Boat headquarters that the fast convoy HX229 out of Halifax, with forty ships, was on the evening of March 13th in a position south-east of Cape Race and steering on the course of 89 degrees. The following day 'B' Service again turned up trumps with the information that the slow convoy SC122 from Sydney, Nova Scotia, with no less than sixty ships, had received orders to sail to a specified point then make course across the Atlantic on 67 degrees. The U-Boats which had taken part in the action against HX228 were at that time sweeping westwards in a patrol line. Twelve were formed into the *Raubgraf* group and were immediately ordered onto a course where they might intercept the more easterly of the two convoys, SC122. Their first sighting came on the evening of March 15th, when a destroyer was soon steaming eastwards, but that proved to have nothing to do with the convoy. Other U-Boats in the region were formed into two groups. Fourteen boats recently relieved from operations against other convoys, together with four U-Boats recently refuelled and re-stocked in the Biscay bases, were formed into the *Sturmer* group. Nine others, plus two boats fresh from Biscay, formed the *Dranger* group.

Then on March 16th a solitary U-653, which was limping back to base after an engine failure, suddenly sighted one or other of the convoys. From its reported position, Doenitz believed it to be SC122, and the whole *Raubgraf* group, together with eleven boats of the *Sturmer* group and two others which had just been replenished from a 'milch cow', were ordered to intercept it.

The erroneous belief that this was SC122 was based largely on the misinterpretation by 'B' Service of a signal from the British Admiralty which led them to believe that HX229 could not be in this region. The signal told HX229 to alter its planned course and sail north to avoid the concentration of U-Boats. But, it seems, it must have been a 'red herring' put out by the Admiralty. The ruse worked, for the remaining *Sturmer* and the eleven *Dranger* group U-Boats were ordered north to intercept.

In fact the sighted convoy was the fast HX229, and it was left to the *Raubgraf* group to attack it. Penetration was easy, since the whole convoy of eleven columns of ships was defended by only four destroyers and a single corvette. At 10.00 pm that night (March 16th) U-603 fired three FAT torpedoes and one conventional torpedo, and the battle was on. Running on its pre-arranged course among the merchantmen, one of the FAT torpedoes struck home, and the Norwegian freighter *Elin K* was hit and sunk. Soon afterwards U-753, working from the starboard side of the convoy, fired two conventional torpedoes and two FATs and brought to a halt the steamers *Zaanland* from the Netherlands, and *James Oglethorpe* from the United States. Immediately all but one of the destroyers dropped back to attend to survivors and while the last remaining destroyer churned futilely up and down in front of the convoy trying to stem the onslaught, the U-Boats were able to choose their target. Lt Strelow in U-453 on the port side torpedoed and stopped the steamer *William Eustis*, but failed to sink it. Strelow withdrew to re-load his bow

torpedo tubes and at 2.30 pm fired off four – two FATs and two type E torpedoes with magnetic ignition. A long interval later Strelow heard four explosions which he and his delighted crew took to be hits on four ships. His claims were in fact more properly due to U-91, which was operating on the opposite side of the convoy and had fired two torpedoes at point blank range into the leading starboard side ship, the American freighter *Harry Luckenbach*. Strelow's other two explosions were either detonations at the end of his torpedoes' runs, or depth charge attacks on one of the other U-Boats.

Also on the starboard side was U-600, which managed to stay completely unobserved while firing torpedoes from all its five tubes. The first struck the British steamer *Nariva*, two struck the American *Irene du Pont*, and then a fourth hit the whaling ship *Southern Princess*. U-616, trying to penetrate the columns of the convoy from the front, suddenly came face to face with the single destroyer escort. Lt-Cdr Koitschka fired four torpedoes at it from close range, and remained undetected. He felt certain he had a sunken destroyer to his credit, but at the last moment it was favoured by chance and turned away out of the path of the four torpedoes.

Still sailing north, hoping to intercept the supposed convoy upon which the *Raubgraf* group was already beginning to inflict such losses, *Sturmer* group and the eleven boats of *Dranger* group happened to come upon the slow convoy SC122 during the night of March 16th. This convoy, 120 miles ahead of the Halifax convoy, was now down to fifty-two ships, two having returned to New York and six having taken shelter at Halifax when a westerly gale developed. It was more powerfully escorted than HX229, with two destroyers, five corvettes, and a frigate. That night the escorts succeeded in fending off the attacks of all but one U-Boat, U-338, under Lt-Cdr Kinzel, but the results which he achieved were extraordinary. Kinzel began by firing two pairs of two torpedoes in the front of the seventh column. His first pair hit the *Kingsbury* and the *King Gruffydd* and both sank within an hour. His second pair both hit the Dutch steamer *Alderamin* and she too soon sank. U-338 then turned away and fired a stern torpedo at the convoy commodore's ship *Glenapp*. The torpedo's depth setting caused it to pass beneath the *Glenapp*, after which it passed between ships in the ninth, tenth, and eleventh columns, and eventually hit and sank the *Fort Cedar Lake*.

It was only from reports sent in by U-Boats on the morning of March 17th that Doenitz eventually learned that the two separate convoys had been located and attacked. Rather than direct any of his U-Boats against either convoy specifically,

Doomed and sinking fast by the stern, a
U-Boat, victim of a US Avenger from an
escort carrier, bows out of the battle.
30 of its crew were rescued

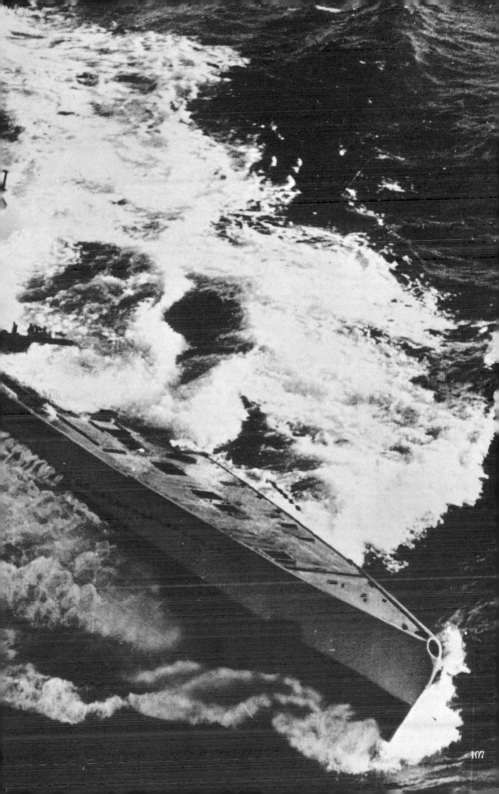

in the confused situation Doenitz gave them all permission to attack any targets which presented themselves. By that day Liberator bombers flown from the bases in Iceland and Northern Ireland were able to reach the slower convoy and during daylight hours all but one of the twenty-eight boats in contact were forced to dive and fall behind. Only Kinzel in U-338 managed to keep in touch, and he followed his achievements of the previous night by sinking the steamer *Granville* early that afternoon.

But HX229 was not yet within range of long distance air cover, and was still widely dispersed and badly escorted after the panic of the first night. The attack on it continued during the day, and *James Oglethorpe* and *William Eustis*, both already damaged, were despatched by U-91. U-384 sank the British steamer *Coracero*, and U-631 the Dutch *Terkolei*. This convoy was now passing through the same waters that the slow convoy had sailed during the night, and several merchantmen drifting helplessly without crews were sunk. It was this kind of double attack, with merchant ships being claimed by both the boat that first hit it and the boat that eventually sank it, which contributed greatly to the over-estimation of the total tonnage sunk in any convoy attack.

Late that afternoon, HX229 also received the welcome support of Liberator bombers, which forced all submarines still in touch to dive for cover. In addition, many of them were now out of fuel or torpedoes and were sailing back to base or to make contact with a submarine tanker.

After dark that night the U-Boats again took up the attack on SC122. Lt-Cdr Bahr in U-305 fired two pairs of torpedoes and scored hits on two ships, the *Zouave* and *Port Auckland*, before being forced to dive by a menacing destroyer. When U-305 surfaced at 11.41pm the *Zouave* had sunk and *Port Auckland* was drifting out of control. Bahr put another torpedo into it, which sent up a huge cloud of black smoke from the engine room, and then U-338 also joined in and torpedoed the ship. Finally drifting broadside on to the mounting waves, Port Auckland was pounded so severely that she broke up and sank. The slow convoy was better protected during daylight hours on March 18th, by both the air escorts and the surface vessels, and by the improving visibility, and no U-Boats could operate during that day.

HX229 was less well defended, and at 3.52pm U-221 broke through the convoy's meagre protective screen in an underwater attack, fired all his five torpedo tubes, and sank the freighter *Walter Q. Gresham* and the refrigerator ship *Canadian Star*.

During that night, HX229 had closed up so much on the slower convoy that the two appeared to be sailing as one great fleet, and it became almost impossible to determine

against which of the two any U-Boat was operating. As the air escorts flew away for the night the attacks began again, though with varying success. U-666 and U-441 each launched five torpedoes, but the range was too great for accuracy and all missed. U-608 fired a treble salvo at the destroyer *Highlander* but they also missed. U-666 was luckier in her next attack, when she torpedoed the freighter *Carras*. She failed to sink it immediately, but the crew abandoned their vessel and it was ultimately lost.

By the morning of March 20th the air support was growing so strong that the U-Boats were suffering a harassment they could no longer bear. U-384 was sunk by a Liberator bomber. The others were ordered to break off the action, and attack only stragglers or ships already damaged. The steamer *Matthew Luckenbach* and the still floating *Carras* were sunk after being separated from the convoy.

U-384 was the only U-Boat destroyed during the operation, although two others, U-631 and U-441, were depth charged when they persisted in pursuing the convoys after the withdrawal had been ordered, and they had to make for base with severe damage.

In the five days and nights during which that furious battle raged, twenty-one ships were sunk – a total of 141,000 tons. It was a huge victory for the U-Boats, and it set the seal on a spectacularly successful month. In the first three weeks of March more than half a million tons of shipping were sunk, and when the British Admiralty later came to evaluate the significance of those weeks, they concluded that 'the Germans never came so near to disrupting communications between the New World and the Old as in the first twenty days of March 1943'.

Apart from the magnitude of the sinkings themselves, the bleakest feature of the episode was that two thirds of all the vessels sunk were sailing in convoy. Had the U-Boats in fact succeeded in breaking the convoy system? Would they force the Allies to abandon it? If so, what other system could possibly replace it? The 'happy time' off the American coast had shown the carnage that resulted when ships were sailed independently.

For a time, it appeared to the U-Boat command that victory in the Battle of the Atlantic was in their hands. If the succeeding weeks yielded results as overwhelmingly in their favour as that mighty duel, the lifeline between the Allies would be strangled, their supplies of raw materials, fuel and food cut off, and the build-up of armaments and troops for the threatened invasion of Europe thwarted. If the pendulum continued to swing in their favour, the U-Boats would gradually, but with inexorable certainty, lead the way to victory for the Axis powers.

Victory into defeat

In the succeeding weeks, however, there were to be no comparable victories. Doenitz mounted a number of actions against convoys not only on the North Atlantic route, but also on the more southerly route from America to North Africa, as well as in the Caribbean and off the coast of the United States. But none produced more than moderate sinkings.

At the end of March an incident of the utmost significance occurred when a U-Boat reported sighting an aircraft carrier sailing with a convoy. Aircraft flown off it prevented that and other U-Boats from operating against the merchant ships. The carrier *Audacity* had been used on the Gibraltar route in 1941, and had been sunk by a U-Boat in December of that year, but this was the first use of aircraft carriers with the trans-Atlantic convoys. Soon afterwards, many of the U-Boats working on those routes were forced by lack of fuel to return to the Biscay bases, leaving only one group to consolidate the victory of less than two weeks earlier. This last group also, during an attack on the next eastbound convoy out of Halifax, reported an aircraft carrier operating within the ranks of the convoy, which flew off enough aircraft to defy all attempts by the U-Boats at taking up their best position, with the result that only six ships could be sunk.

It was with these aircraft carriers that the Allies had now, quite suddenly, succeeded in closing the 'air gap'.

Nor was that all. From the end of March the Allies at last managed to organise in adequate numbers the 'Support Groups' of surface escorts which they had planned in September and October of 1942. At that time, in respect of both the support groups and the aircraft carriers, the higher priority of defending the North African invasion forces in Operation Torch had prevented their introduction on the North Atlantic convoy routes. Now they could be introduced into the Battle of the Atlantic, and a terror they were to the U-Boats. Small flotillas of escort vessels with highly trained and experienced crews, they were not committed to a single convoy, but were free to race across the oceans to reinforce the escort of any merchant fleet threatened by a U-Boat attack. The U-Boats found to their cost that the advent of the support groups meant that escort vessels were no longer forced to leave off an attack on a U-Boat to return to the convoy's protection. They could persist in their depth charging, and the result was all too often the patch of oil, the piece of furniture or the odd item of food or clothing, that told of the end of the U-Boat.

The British produced a further trick by improvising carrier borne air support in the form of grain carriers and tankers fitted out with a flight deck, to carry three or four Swordfish aircraft. Since the Swordfish

could land on the deck and refuel for another take-off, these Merchant Aircraft Carriers were a considerably greater threat to the U-Boats that the Catapult Aircraft Merchantmen which had been used with their single disposable Hurricane in the summer of 1941.

After the 'vacuum' in the North Atlantic caused by so many boats arriving at base simultaneously, they began to return in the middle of April, at last, in ever-increasing numbers, and events promised to show whether the great successes of March would be repeated. The first convoy against which the new concentration could work was HX233, passing on the southern route only 400 miles north of the Azores. The weather was calm and the sea still, so that the escorts, reinforced by a support group, had little difficulty in picking up radar contact with the U-Boats. The encounter came out even: one ship of 7,487 tons sank, and U-176 destroyed.

The next fast convoy, HX234, was routed far to the north specifically to avoid running into that pack of U-Boats, but Doenitz had been able to form another group from those newly out of Biscay, and for three days from April 21st an attack was mounted. This time, however, the U-Boats complained of adverse weather conditions of a different kind, with fog, snow, and hail to interrupt their visibility. Suddenly it seemed as if the U-Boats were demanding a gentle breeze

and clear visibility before they could start work. Only five ships were sunk from the convoy, at a cost of two U-Boats.

By the end of April enough U-Boats were amassed in the area to the south of Greenland to form up several large packs lying in wait in the path of the convoy ONS5, which 'B' Service had reported to be east of Cape Farewell. Then the weather broke again, and both the convoy and the U-Boats were blown into disorder, making an attack impossible for several days. But by the night of May 4th the storm had given way to calm and the convoy had almost collected together. The U-Boats struck. That night five merchantmen went down, and on the following day four more ships were sunk, despite the convoy escorts and a powerful support group. When darkness fell the U-Boats continued the fight, and in more than two dozen attempted torpedo strikes, pushed the merchant crews to the limit of their nerve and endurance. But astonishingly they sank not a single ship. On the other hand, the escorts went about their work with unprecedented energy and skill, and that same night sank four U-Boats. By the time the convoy reached the safety of the North American ports, twelve of their numbers were lost, but the operation had also cost seven U-Boats.

Despite these unsatisfactory results, Doenitz immediately deployed his forces for another attack, but the outcome was no

more encouraging. The fast convoy HX237 sailed under the protection of the aircraft carrier *Biter*, and the U-Boats succeeded in sinking only three ships. On the other side, three U Boats were destroyed, one by *Biter's* aircraft, another by the shorebased aircraft, and the third by both shorebased aircraft and surface vessels carrying out a combined attack. As soon as the strength of aircraft patrolling from the shore increased, *Biter* was detached to support the slow convoy SC129, which another pack of U-Boats was threatening. This time two ships were sunk, but the escorts in return destroyed two U-Boats and damaged several others.

For the moment, the score was even, but the downward trend for the U-Boats continued, and they received a drubbing at the hands of the escort to their next intended victims, the ships of SC130. Four packs attacked between May 15th and 20th. They failed to sink even a single ship, but five U-Boats were lost.

As events turned out, SC130 was the last North Atlantic convoy to be seriously threatened by the U-Boats, for Doenitz could bear losses of this magnitude no longer. Faced with the proven ability of enemy aircraft to locate his U-Boats by radar, and the skill of the surface vessels in following up sightings, Doenitz knew that, temporarily at least, he would have to retire from the combat. Nor, until the

power of his U-Boats to accept and reply to this new challenge was vastly increased, would there be any going back. On May 24th, Doenitz withdrew his U-Boats from the convoy routes.

It was on that day that the Battle of the Atlantic was won and lost.

To U-Boat command, it was baffling that after such a decisive victory against convoys HX229 and SC122 in March, fortunes in the Battle of the Atlantic should have been so suddenly and completely reversed. In a period of only eight weeks, the promise of victory for the U-Boats had been turned into the actuality of failure. They had been thrown on the defensive, and the escorts had fastened an unbreakable grip on the situation.

In retrospect, however, it is clear that what the U-Boat arm regarded at the time as a pattern of developing ascendancy should have been seen, if all the relevant factors had been apparent, as the final, spirited struggle of a declining force. For the Allies, even before March, had started to introduce into the conflict a number of measures which spelled the end of the U-Boats' days of glory.

In the first place, their successes in the operations in North Africa had made available for the convoy routes great numbers of escort ships, and released hundreds of men eager to take part in this battle against the U-Boats. The Germans,

The escorts strike back; a U-Boat is depth charged from the air

by contrast, although their building programme progressed with undramatic steadiness, had nothing like a comparable number of U-Boats ready to throw into the fight to preserve the balance of their superiority. In addition, the Allies had applied their most able brains to the problem of supplying those men and fitting those ships with the most advanced and effective equipment which military ingenuity could devise, while the Germans, with uncharacteristic lassitude, had neglected to employ to the full their capacity for scientific invention, had failed to keep pace with the Allies, and were now several months behind in the race for technical supremacy. Before they could begin to catch up, the Allies, fresh from their triumph in North Africa, could start to turn from the brink of defeat in that March and devote their increasing resources to a massive attempt to finish once and for all the threat of the U-Boats.

It was in the Bay of Biscay that a few events early in the year could and should have told Doenitz what to expect in the wider battle. There, as early as February, U-519 was caught on the surface and sunk by an American Liberator bomber, apparently after having no indication from its search receiver that it had been discovered. A few weeks later U-333 was also attacked, this time by a Wellington bomer, but it had the better of the encounter and shot down the aircraft. It confirmed that no prior warning

of the aircraft's radar had been gained from the search receiver, and from then on the U-Boat arm began to suspect the existence of an important new surface location device in the possession of the British air patrols. In fact it was the new 10 centimetre radar set, which had been in too short supply at the end of 1942, but which was now coming into use in Allied aircraft.

After investigating the evidence Doenitz came to the conclusion that the Allies had indeed acquired long range radar equipment, and on March 3rd he therefore ordered all U-Boats to stay submerged as soon as they became aware of radar transmissions and to stay submerged for 30 minutes. The new radar was, of course, so effective against their inadequate search receivers that the damage had almost invariably been done, and they had already been located and were under attack. In any case, the order, issued only as a desperate emergency measure, served the Allied cause by eliminating the U-Boat from the battle for as long as it was submerged.

Their growing disadvantage was illustrated again in March, when on the 22nd of the month another U-Boat was sunk and one damaged, and in April when U-376 was lost and another was damaged. Then in May the sinkings of U-Boats in the Bay of Biscay began to rise alarmingly. In the first week U-332, U-109, and U-663 were all sunk by marauding aircraft during daylight, and

112

on May 15 a Halifax bomber sank a 'milch cow', U-463, on the way to the Atlantic routes with its valuable cargo for the operational submarines. These attacks were too much for Doenitz. Recollecting the successful self-defence action of U-333 in shooting down its attacker during March, and seeing that the order to submerge was having little effect against the new kind of radar, he ordered all the U-Boats to stay on the surface and fight it out with the aircraft. Even if they could not shoot it down, their fire power might prove enough to divert it and force it to drop its bombs inaccurately.

He also ordered some U-Boats to be especially equipped with heavy fire power, in an effort to put the British Coastal Command on the defensive by persuading them that air attacks over the Bay were too expensive to continue. The first of these new 'aircraft traps', U-441, sailed from Brest on May 22nd, bristling with two four barrelled 2cm cannon and a semi-automatic 3.7cm cannon, and two days later it proved its value as 'bait' by drawing the attack of a Sunderland boat. The encounter was at least a partial success. U-441 shot down the Sunderland, but the aircraft managed to drop its bombs before crashing and U-441 had to return to base for repairs.

By June, since Doenitz had withdrawn from the Atlantic, the Bay of Biscay had become the focal point of the conflict. On June 8th Lt Feindt in U-758, another converted and heavily armed U-Boat, fought with several aircraft from an aircraft carrier. The first to attack got badly shot up for its trouble. Two others fired off ineffective bursts from a healthy range, then another attacked and the U-Boat shot it down. Two others were damaged before Feindt, with three of his guns damaged and eleven men wounded, decided to dive.

Following his success, other U-Boats were fitted with extra armaments, and in order to bring the maximum possible fire power to bear on the attacking aircraft, they were ordered to sail in twos and threes. In this way the fundamental advantage of a U-Boat's design was thrown overboard, and they became simply surface fighting vessels. The move rendered them immune for a short time, but by mid-June the escorts had found the answer to that tactic and replied in kind. When they sighted a U-Boat, they circled way off until reinforcements arrived, although not so far away that the U-Boat could dive and escape submerged. Then they mounted a concerted attack from every direction at once. A few attacks of this kind pushed up the incidence of damage and destruction and showed that the 'stand and fight it out' method was failing to pay off, and the U-Boats were soon ordered to revert to their old practice of making the Biscay passage submerged and only surfacing for the mini-

With persistence and accuracy, an
Avenger puts paid to a U-Boat. The wake
left as the U-Boat writhes to escape is
clearly visible

Under attack from a B-25 bomber, U-Boat
suffers depth charging and cannon fire

A Halifax scores a hit; the U-Boat sank within three minutes

another Liberator sank U-628. Two days later U-535 fell victim to a Liberator, and on July 7th yet another Liberator mounted an attack on a group of seven U-Boats, with rockets, depth charges, and an acoustic torpedo, and sank U-514. On July 7th, 8th, and 9th U-951, U-232, and U-435, respectively, were sunk off the coast of Portugal by aircraft flying from the bases at Gibraltar and Morocco. And so, with fierce and relentless fighting, the destruction of U-Boats went on. Nor was it only the British sea and air patrols which took part in this slaughter. In July two United States aircraft carriers, *Core* and *Santee*, turned up, each with three destroyer escorts, in the waters off the Azores, to join the *Bogue*, already patrolling there. Between July 13th and 16th they sank four U-Boats between them, on July 23rd *Bogue* alone sank two more, and on July 30th aircraft from *Santee* raised the tally to seven. It was on July 30th, also, that the British accidentally located two 'milch cows' and another U-Boat sailing in a group. The sheer quantity of air and sea offensive which the British threw into the attack illustrates both their determination to confirm their superiority in the U-Boat war and the vast forces which were now becoming available to them. No less than six aircraft, plus the 2nd Escort Group under Captain Walker, pounced on the three wretched U-Boats. With their meagre armaments the U-Boats gave the aircraft a certain amount of punishment but in the end all three were destroyed.

On August 1st a Sunderland attacked and sank U-454, but the Sunderland itself crashed into the sea. Later that day another Sunderland sank U-383, and the next day U-706 and U-106 went down. This appalling destruction left Doenitz no alternative but to recall six other U-Boats then on course out of the Bay of Biscay and cancel all group sailings for the time being. This decision, on August 2nd, followed the loss of nineteen U-Boats out of eighty-six which attempted to cross the Bay and make the waters of the open Atlantic, but it served the immediate purpose by reducing substantially the numbers of U-Boats sunk during the coming month.

As a more permanent answer to the superiority which the Allies were now clearly and quickly establishing in the battle for command of the sea, Doenitz in the late summer of 1943 turned his attention to the possibilities of a counter offensive being made feasible by German developments in the technical field. On July 30th he elucidated to Hitler, himself now somewhat worried about the way the war was going, the high hopes he had that some of the scientific ideas now coming into operation might revive the flagging fortunes of his unhappy U-Boat arm.

Important technical advances were at that time in the offing in almost all fields of

mum possible time in order to recharge their batteries.

The need to take a decision of this kind was a clear enough indication that the U-Boats had not only been banished from the Atlantic but had been thrown soundly on the defensive in the region of their own bases.

With less call on their services in the Atlantic, several groups of anti-submarine surface vessels appeared in the outer approaches to the Bay and began working in close co-operation with the radar carrying aircraft. As soon as a U-Boat surfaced at night to charge its batteries, the long range radar would come into its own, and the surface vessel would be on the way to deal with it. While the British thus developed close and effective inter-service co-operation, Doenitz was severely handicapped by his own shortage of supporting aircraft, and also by his lack of surface vessels attached to the U-Boat arm.

On July 2nd a series of actions began in the Bay of Biscay which was to mark that month as the most disastrous yet for U-Boat command. Shortly after sailing from Bordeaux that day, U-462, a 'milch cow' due to supply U-Boats operating off the South African coast, was attacked from the air, and so badly damaged that she had to return to base. That night a Leigh Light Liberator surprised U-126 and promptly sank it, and then the following morning

Swimming under water and working on the outside of a submerged U-boat were part of the crew's job

U-Boat activity – their speed under water, their strike effectiveness, and above all their ability to foil the escorts' radar location equipment.

The most important in the summer of 1943 was considered to be radar warning, and a Naval Headquarters Scientific Directorate was set up under Professor Kuepfmueller to tackle the problem. In the early days of its use, Doenitz's scientific advisers expressed great scepticism at the possibility of the British possessing a device fundamentally different from the one and a half metre set to which the warning search receivers had initially provided a complete answer. The new ten centimetre set, for a time, had them baffled. Their difficulty was not alleviated by their ready acceptance of a story from a captured British pilot, who managed to convince his captors that it was no new radar, but simply the emission of signals from their own search receivers, which enabled the British to home onto a surfaced U-Boat. By the time the German scientists woke up to the use of ten centimetre radar sets, and set about inventing a receiver which would pick up new frequencies, 1944 was well under way, and the gap in this sphere of the technical battle had widened.

German scientists were rather more inventive in countering the asdic, by inventing a chemical bubble-producing agent. Dropped in a container from a sub-

merged U-boat, this device, known as a 'bold', produced a mass of bubbles which reflected the asdic's beam in exactly the same way as the boat itself, and proved a useful decoy.

Doenitz hoped and expected that the efficiency of his U-Boats in sinking merchant ships would be greatly improved by the introduction of the new acoustic torpedo. Neither the contact firing pistol nor the magnetic pistol had proved ideal in combat conditions, since the margin for error was too great. Originally their acoustic replacements, which could 'home' onto the sound of an enemy ship's engines, were planned for the autumn of 1944 but the programme had been forced ahead at such a rate that the first U-Boats were able to receive the weapon during the second half of August 1943. But supplies were still short, and at that time each boat could have only four of the new 'Zaunkoenig' (Wren) torpedoes.

The strengthening of Allied radar-equipped escort forces also heightened the need for a submarine which could operate more efficiently at greater speeds under water. The new Walter U-Boat, with its hydrogen peroxide fuel, was on the way, but with such a radically new invention, development and testing would take time, and large numbers of Walter boats could not be expected to become operational before 1945. In the meantime, Doenitz was working on the introduction of a compromise solution, a new boat with the streamlined hull of the Walter design and with a vastly increased quantity of electric batteries to drive orthodox underwater motors. Its most important version, Type XXI, would displace 1,600 tons, achieve a maximum surface speed of 15½ knots, and could cruise submerged for 110 miles at 10 knots. More important, in underwater attacks it would be able to strike in fast bursts lasting up to an hour at 17½ knots, which, considering the maximum 5 or 6 knots of its predecessors, was a major breakthrough. A smaller version of 232 tons, Type XXIII, with a submerged speed of 12½ knots, was also planned for use in coastal waters. Hitler, gravely disturbed at recent developments on the U-Boat front, gave priority for a building programme of twenty-two Type XXI boats and ten Type XXIII boats monthly, and their construction began towards the end of 1943, in yards at Hamburg, Bremen, and Danzig, where they were prefabricated in eight sections for assembly later. Doenitz's relations with the Fuehrer, far more cordial than those of his predecessor, were beginning to pay off already.

Finally there was the 'schnorkel'. In November 1942, at a technical conference in Paris, Professor Walter had suggested the possibility of fitting U-Boats with a ventilating apparatus through which the boat could draw fresh air, for both the crew and the diesels, and expel exhaust fumes, while it remained submerged. Not only would the U-Boat be able to achieve high under-water speeds on its conventional engines, but the absence of a conning tower above the surface would render it virtually immune from long range radar detection. When it was first discovered in a Dutch U-Boat captured during the invasion of that country in 1940, German scientists had paid scant regard to the usefulness of this device, but the early summer of 1943 had made the implementation of some such idea absolutely essential, and in July trials were going ahead with great promise of success.

Until technical progress should alter the complexion of the U-Boat war, however, Doenitz and his subordinates faced the future with dismay. It was in June that Doenitz, his own personal confidence for once shaken by events, underwent a period of earnest soul-searching regarding the question of whether he should call the U-Boats out of the conflict altogether. It was a shattering loss of heart in an admiral who throughout the war had regarded his U-Boat arm as the critical instrument in ensuring success against the Allies, and who, such a short time earlier, felt himself on the verge of seeing all his hopes come to fruition. But now all the factors which had thrown the U-Boats on the defensive – the numbers of escorts, their techniques, the increase in air support, and not least the sudden alteration in May of British cyphers which 'B' Service had so far failed to break – led him to the conclusion that if he continued to operate the U-Boat arm in its present condition, before the new designs and improved weapons were available, he would only be sending hundreds of young men to a certain death, and throwing dozens of U-Boats into an uneven battle from which large numbers would never return.

On the other hand, to call off the U-Boat war might have the direst consequences. As soon as the Allies realised that U-Boat activities had ceased, they would be free to divert vast resources of manpower and materials away from the shipping lanes to operate against Germany and the other Axis powers elsewhere. Not only that, but the war material crossing the oceans in convoys would arrive certainly and unmolested. Any single success which the U-Boats might score, however great the cost, would reduce the Allied capability in the invasion they were mounting. If the U-Boats failed to go on, even on the increasingly unfavourable terms, the result would be a greater burden for the other arms of the fighting services to bear. Not least in importance, any pause in the activities of the U-Boat crews, while they waited for the new boats to come out of the yards, could only undermine their morale and drain them of the one quality which they had so far shown to be theirs in valuable abundance – their determination to fight.

There was no alternative, the U-Boat war had to go on.

After the defeat in the Atlantic and the decision at the end of May to withdraw from operations against the shipping routes there, Doenitz was left with a considerable force of U-Boats to deploy elsewhere. Those which were still adequately fuelled for further attacks, about sixteen boats, were formed into a group west of the Azores, but they had no success. While a convoy passed tantalisingly close to their formation, the aircraft carrier Bogue flew off aircraft which attacked and sank U-217.

With his remaining boats Doenitz had to look to other theatres and revive the old practice of attacking the enemy's 'soft spots' where the escorts were weak and the attacks unexpected. Of the boats which succeeded in running the gauntlet of the British patrols in the Bay of Biscay, seven reached American coastal waters after refuelling from a U-tanker off the Azores, but they achieved little, in the face of strong air escorts, particularly from aircraft carriers, and unexpectedly heavy surface escorts. It was a surface vessel which sank U-521 off Cape Hatteras. All boats taking

Refuelling at sea; valuable fuel from a U-tanker extended the U-Boat's radius and time on operations.

part in these operations were given freedom to roam over large areas, to avoid working together, in the hopes that those responsible for anti-submarine measures would not be inspired to build up a heavy concentration of escorts against them. But these hopes were ill-founded. In a short time their arrival led to a stiffening of defensive forces, and the U-Boats were soon hounded out of those waters altogether.

Off West Africa a similar story evolved. After individual actions the U-Boats did in fact come together for an attack on a convoy sailing north, but the escorts defended it so skilfully that only one ship was sunk. Further to the south, the U-Boats achieved moderate successes off the Cape of Good Hope, with the sinking of several ships sailing independently. Then the seven which were operating there took the battle once more into the Indian Ocean, where they refuelled from a tanker off Madagascar. They sank ten ships in June, and notched up the respectable total of seventeen ships of 97,214 tons in July. On June 9th, with so many boats now free, Doenitz sent nine others to reinforce the original seven, together with two U-tankers. To avoid the dangers of crossing the Bay of Biscay, they sailed from German bases and took the northerly route round the north of Scot-

land and between the Shetland Islands and Iceland. One U-Boat, U-200, was sunk in the early stages of the passage, and on the journey south the remainder suffered extensively at the hands of the United States carrier-borne aircraft and patrols flown from England. But five survived to reach the Cape of Good Hope and made the passage into the Indian Ocean, where they refuelled from a tanker south of Madagascar and spread out over the Arabian Sea and the Indian Ocean to work alongside the eight Japanese submarines patrolling that area, while the earlier boats began the long voyage home. By the end of the year the U-Boats in the Indian Ocean had, with nominal help from their Japanese colleagues, sunk fifty-seven ships of 337,169 tons, mainly at the entrance to the Persian Gulf and the Red Sea, where ships sailing independently and without escort were forced to concentrate. With no more than seven U-Boats at any time operating there, these successes gave Doenitz considerable cause for gratification. On the other hand, the passage through the Atlantic was becoming more and more dangerous, and a number of boats destined as reinforcements in the Indian Ocean were destroyed before ever reaching the Cape of Good Hope.

Last throw against the supply lines

At the end of August, Doenitz was able to relax his order of August 2nd forbidding the sailing of any U-Boats, and after a three months absence, nine of them took the fight once more out into the waters of the Atlantic. Doenitz pinned high hopes on their new equipment, the improved radar search receiver, the acoustic homing torpedo, and the heavily reinforced anti-aircraft armaments which they all, not only the 'aircraft traps', now carried. Early in September this first group was followed by a second group of thirteen from the Biscay bases, and six others from ports in Norway and Germany.

In the Bay of Biscay, the new measures seemed for a time to have given the U-Boats the advantage. They stayed submerged except when surfacing to recharge their batteries, and they hugged close the Spanish coastline as far as Cape Finisterre. Only one from the group of thirteen, U-669, was sunk by the Allied air patrols, and even by the end of September only one other had been added. Their 'Bay Offensive' sorties, on the other hand, cost the Allies no less than thirteen aircraft.

After their long passage across the Bay, the boats re-fuelled from a tanker, and took up their positions in a patrol line to intercept slow convoys sailing to America, with orders to strike at the escorts first, then deal with the defenceless convoys later. The west-bound convoy ONS18, consisting of twenty-seven ships, including a Merchant Aircraft Carrier, with an escort of eight vessels, left Britain on September 12th. It was followed on September 15th by forty ships of ON202, with a six-strong escort. On September 16th, when nineteen U-Boats formed up into a line running roughly north-south and more or less on longitude 25 degrees. the scene was set for a new trial of strength by the two sides, the first since each had been able to take advantage of their respective technical developments.

The exchange of radio messages entailed in forming the U-Boats into their operational line had, contrary to the earnest hopes of U-Boat command, been intercepted by the British Admiralty in the submarine tracking room and on September 16th a support group was sent to lend valuable strength to the escort of ONS18.

The first contact came at dawn on September 19th, when a Liberator flying ahead of the convoy sank U-341, before the U-Boats had even sighted their enemy. That night U-270 was the first to see the ships, and it and one other U-Boat opened up the proceedings with a preliminary attack. But this was merely the sounding out of the escorts' strength, and nothing was sunk. The next night, September 20th, the attacks began in earnest. The faster convoy, ON202, had caught up with the slow one and was only a few miles to the north, and it was on that convoy that the first losses were inflicted. Following Doenitz's order the U-Boats turned first on the escorts, and the frigate *Lagan* was soon on the way home with severe damage from an acoustic torpedo. Then two merchant ships were sunk, but early that morning Liberators from Iceland replied by sinking U-338. Ironically, this was with an acoustic torpedo, dropped from the aircraft. For just as the U-Boat arm felt they had come up with the answer to the enemy's technical superiority, the Allies brought into service their own version of the same idea. In addition, they had kept one step ahead, assumed that the Germans would also be developing this type of torpedo, and applied themselves to the problem of producing an antidote. When they did hit on the right idea, it was of stunning simplicity. They merely towed a noise-producing machine astern of the ship. Since it made more noise than the ship's own engines, the acoustic torpedo homed on to it, and exploded a safe distance away. As yet, however, that refinement had not been introduced.

During the day, in a repetition of the pattern which developed in March, the two convoys merged together and sailed as one. On that earlier occasion, the principal result of the manoeuvre was to increase the number of ships from which the U-Boats could pick off their targets. But this time the effect was to double the strength of the escort. That night between them they frustrated three attacks on the convoy itself. A bigger battle then began behind the merchant ships between the escorts and the U-Boats. At 8pm an acoustic torpedo blew up the stern of the destroyer *St. Croix*, and an hour later it was sunk with a conventional torpedo. At 10.30pm another acoustic torpedo sank the corvette *Polyanthus*.

The next day, September 21st, fog came down and for the time being put an end to the U-Boats' activities. They surfaced, and drove on hard ahead of the convoy. During the periods when the fog lifted they were subjected to close scrutiny by the aircraft but succeeded in keeping them beyond accurate bombing range by the energetic use of their new A.A. weapons. When night fell, the attacks began again, but the escorts managed to keep the U-Boats away from the merchantmen. In fact, the next mortal blow was dealt by the destroyer *Keppel*, which rammed and sank U-229 early in the morning of September 22nd. The day produced more fog, and no further sinkings. That night, a U-Boat fired an acoustic torpedo at the destroyer *Itchen* and sank it, sending to their deaths all but three of the men on board, who included the survivors of the *St. Croix* and *Polyanthus*.

After that the U-Boats began to come into their own. They at last succeeded, at 2.20 on the morning of September 23rd, in penetrating the cordon of destroyers, and within four hours had sunk four merchant vessels. Then fog came down again, and that, plus the ubiquitous air escort, caused Doenitz to call off the operation. He considered it a success. The U-Boat commanders claimed to have sunk twelve destroyers with acoustic torpedoes, and nine ships from the convoys with conventional ones. It later became clear that their normally exaggerated claims regarding successes became even more fanciful on the introduction of the acoustic torpedo. This largely arose from the need for U-Boats to dive immediately they had fired. If they failed to do so, the acoustic torpedo had an unpleasant habit of turning round, immediately it left the tube, and making for the noisiest thing in the vicinity – their own diesel engines. They were unable ever to see a strike, and from their positions under water, terminal explosions and distant depth charge detonations were all too often taken as, and reported as, successes.

In fact, the nineteen U-Boats which had formed the pack had sunk six merchant ships and three escorts, and damaged one other escort. Three U-Boats failed to survive, and three others were damaged.

Elated with the misleading reports, and confident that in the acoustic torpedo he had uncovered the answer to his problems, Doenitz formed the remaining boats once more into a line to wait for convoys. It was an unfortunate mistake. Two convoys were diverted around the formation, a third was given a powerful air escort, and the U-Boats did not even see the ships, although the aircraft sank U 279, U-366, and U-389. A fourth convoy, SC143, was contacted on October 8th. Its thirty-nine ships had an escort of nine, and eighteen U-Boats were lined up against it. They succeeded in sinking one destroyer, the *Orkan*, but when, later that day, air escorts arrived, three more U-Boats, U-419, U-643 and U-610, were sunk.

Not until October 15th was another convoy, ON206, sighted in the Atlantic, and the action against it was no more encouraging. An attack by U-Boats that night failed when the escorts forced them to dive deep. Before they could mount any attack the next night, Liberators operating some way from the convoy located with their radar, and sank, U-884 and U-470. On the evening of October 17th U-540 was destroyed in the same way, and soon afterwards U-631 was blown to the surface by a depth charge attack from a corvette, and promptly sunk. A second convoy, ONS20, was following in the wake of the first, and the U-Boats managed to sink one of its merchant ships. The British replied immediately when a Liberator sank U-964 and a frigate sank U-841. The two battles had cost six U-Boats and only one merchant ship.

Results like these were again becoming

A tanker and its cargo of fuel ablaze
after a hit

the rule rather than the exception and Doenitz was continually forced to ponder the question of whether he should call off the U-Boat war altogether. Again he chose not to, and once more formed his boats into line. But as Doenitz tried to meet the new situation by throwing more and more U-Boats against the convoys, his enemy replied by providing stronger and stronger escorts. Of the next four convoys which sailed, not a single ship was sunk. But the surface and air escorts worked in a unison which the Germans, largely because of Goering's pathological unwillingness to co-operate, had never achieved, and between them sank another three U-Boats.

Nor was it only co-operation between the various arms of the British forces that led to the end for so many U-Boats. Among the surface vessels, excellent teamwork to a large extent solved the problems inherent in their barely adequate weapons, and the inventive Captain Walker, now in the sloop *Starling*, was again the inspiration behind many successful attacks. It was in this period that many a U-Boat crew must have died with shocked expressions on their faces, for terrible as it was, the 'ping' of a hunting destroyer's asdic against the hull of the U-Boat had its element of comfort. While it could be heard, there was still a chance of escape, for the destroyer could not yet be close enough to drop depth charges. It was when the 'ping' stopped that the worry really started. Had the contact simply been lost? Or was the destroyer racing directly overhead, and were the depth charges, released over the stern, on their way down? When that silence came, it was time for the U-Boat to squirm and writhe under maximum power to escape those explosions, and throw the destroyer out of contact for good. Now, the 'ping' was continuing, until with utter finality the depth charge exploded and the water came pouring in through the cracked hull. The U-Boat captains had no way of knowing, of course, and no way of telling about it later, but British accounts subsequently showed how Walker had evolved his 'creeping attacks'. He would station one boat directly in front of another. The second destroyer kept the U-Boat in asdic contact, and directed the first along its track and on over it. Carefully computing the U-Boat's distance and speed, the commander of the second boat would signal when he wanted a carpet of depth charges to be dropped from the one in front, timing his signal so that by the time they sank to the U-Boat's depth, it would have sailed on to exactly the right place. If the U-Boat was trying to escape by twisting and turning, the escort at the rear could guide two or three others on to its likely track. The accuracy of the method was almost infallible, the results invariably deadly. Walker, who died from overwork in July 1944, was a worthy

opponent for the best of the U-Boat commanders.

A destroyer acting by itself also had an answer to the problem of lost asdic contact – less elaborate and not quite so accurate – in the form of a device for throwing depth charges out in front of its bows. The earliest version was known as the 'hedgehog', and consisted of a bristling clutch of 24 depth charges, any of which would explode on contact. The advantage was that unless the U-Boat was hit, no explosion took place to disturb the asdic contact, and the hedgehog could be reloaded for another shot.

In the two months of September and October 1943 the U-Boat arm lost no less than twenty-five boats in those new attacks on the North Atlantic convoy routes. Their own achievements were paltry – just nine merchant ships! The end of October, in the event, spelled the end of the wolf pack. Doenitz from that time on dispersed the big concentrations of U-Boats since these evidently appeared to be precisely the kind of target which the escort found most welcome, and formed his resources into small independently acting groups. But even these were not immune from the ever vigilant aircraft. Several groups of two or three U-Boats, formed in the waters to the east of Newfoundland and the south of Greenland, found that almost the moment they showed their periscopes above the water, the aircraft were bearing down and illuminating them. And if the aircraft themselves did not drop bombs and depth charges, the surface escorts would soon be racing over, and the asdic's 'ping' on the hull would start.

As they came out of the building pens, new U-Boats were sent out into the North Atlantic. But it was a futile effort. In November only six merchant ships of 23,000 tons were sunk; in December only seven ships of 48,000 tons. And on those same convoy routes, in those same two months, sixteen U-Boats were destroyed. Compared with the previous March, when in the North Atlantic alone eighty ships of 476,349 tons were sunk in a single month for the loss of only six U-Boats, it was clear which way the war was going.

As the extent of the failure of his renewed effort had begun to emerge in the North Atlantic, Doenitz had tried to redeem the situation by increasing the pressure in other waters. On the southern convoy routes, in the vicinity of the Azores, the United States aircraft carrier *Card* had dealt a severe blow to his hopes by sinking the U-tanker U-422. Another aircraft carrier, *Block Island*, followed this on October 28th by sinking the U-tanker U-220. The U-Boat arm was left with only one U-tanker, U-488, to supply boats for extended operations, and for the sake of its safety, Doenitz withdrew this boat from the areas made so unhealthy by the aircraft carriers and sent it to the comparative safety of the African coast.

It was against the north-south convoys from Freetown and Gibraltar that the main weight of this new pressure was directed. Yet here also the summer of 1943 had seen the Allies slot into place another key piece in the complex inter-locking jigsaw pattern of surface and air anti-submarine measures. In August the Portuguese government, after two years of negotiation, finally signed an agreement with Britain permitting the use of air bases on two islands in the Azores. The British began to occupy their bases on October 8th, and by the 19th of that month the first aircraft were flying anti-U-Boat sorties, giving the Allies blanket air cover over the entire Atlantic ocean north of latitude 30 degrees.

Doenitz, in opposition to them, lined up a group of eight new U-Boats, and enjoyed the reconnaissance facilities of the Luftwaffe, which had agreed to provide a small number of aircraft to co-operate with the U-Boat arm. The opposing forces came into contact for the first time on October 27th when a Focke-Wulf reported a convoy of sixty ships sailing north. At dawn on October 31st, the U-Boats, sweeping south in a line, made their first sighting, and the battle opened. It did not last long. Firstly, U-306 was sunk in a combined effort by a destroyer and a corvette. The U-Boats damaged a merchant vessel, but then one of the U-Boats was herself damaged, and in view of the reported strength of the air cover, which included aircraft from the new Azores bases, U-Boat Command called off the attack.

On November 7th the Focke-Wulfs reported another convoy sailing north, but when the U-Boats made contact they only succeeded in losing one sunk and one damaged, without destroying any ships. On November 16th, the value of having reconnaissance aircraft was put beyond doubt when they reported yet another convoy of sixty-six ships. These were in fact the ships of convoys SL139 from Sierra Leone, and MKS30 from Gibraltar, sailing under a combined escort. Against them Doenitz ordered twenty-six U-Boats into a line, and at 11 a.m. on November 18th they met. The destroyer *Exe* promptly rammed U-333 and sent her limping back to base with severe damage, and then a U-Boat replied in kind, sending the sloop *Chanticleer* home under tow with her stern blown away by an acoustic torpedo. After that the British saturated the area round the convoy with escorts. Hudsons, Fortresses, and Catalinas swarmed above the ships during the day, and after dark Leigh Light Wellingtons came with the threat of illuminating any U-Boats unwise enough to show their periscopes above the surface. U-211 was such a boat: it was immediately sunk. Nine more escort ships arrived on the 19th, making a

total of 19 to protect the merchantmen in two tight cordons. That night, Doenitz again mounted a determined attack, but it was the escorts which drew first blood. U-536 was blown to the surface by depth charges and then subjected to incessant gunfire until she sank. During the following day the battle was carried into the air as the escorting aircraft attacked German reconnaissance planes and shot down two of them. The two sides continued to exchange blow for blow, and it was U-618's turn to strike next, when she brought down a Sunderland flying boat. As night fell on the 20th, the tired combatants still tore into each other with undiminished fury. U-684 shot down a Liberator. A destroyer picked up U-538 on her asdic at 4.30 in the morning, and after six hours of pursuit finally depth charged and sank her.

In all, thirty-one U-Boats had been involved in the attack on the convoys, yet no merchantmen was even harmed. Only one sloop was damaged and two Allied aircraft were shot down, for the loss of three U-Boats destroyed and one damaged.

Having called off that attack, Doenitz, acting with commendable tenacity, lined up another formation of sixteen boats to seek out two more reported convoys, OS59 and KMS30, travelling on a similar route. In this instance the Admiralty was one jump ahead of him. His own formation had already been reported, and an escort was on the way to meet the convoys. The escort group and the U-Boat formation met in a head-on clash, and during the night of November 22nd, while the convoy sailed by out of harm's way, they engaged each other in a skirmish which resulted in the destruction of U-468.

In these busy shipping lanes, there were plenty of targets for the U-Boats, and they switched their efforts continually from one to another, but each time they moved, this same 4th Escort Group moved with them, and it was a relentless pursuit. On November 25th two frigates sank U-600 and followed this on the next day by damaging U-618. By November 27th the 2nd Escort Group under Captain Walker had arrived to help harry the U-Boats, although during that night a Wellington aircraft using a Leigh Light beat them to the next kill by sinking U-542, and on November 29th an aircraft from the United States carrier *Bogue* ended the career of U-86. Only one boat had succeeded in penetrating the screens of escorts, and launching an attack on the convoy, but its torpedoes missed, and it was damaged for its trouble. Understandably, after this accumulation of losses Doenitz called off the campaign in these waters. Behind such a concentration of air and sea escorts, plus the energetic support groups which seemed to be on the scene at any point where the slightest danger threatened, the convoys could burst through the lines of U-Boats

U-849 under attack by a US Naval aircraft. The U-Boat was sunk off the Congo estuary in November 1943.

with almost complete immunity. With the waters of the whole western world proving again too hot for his forces, Doenitz was once more obliged to re-think his strategy for the future. Meanwhile, on the convoy routes, this most disastrous year for the U-Boat arm ended in virtual silence.

A newly overhauled U-Boat is handed back to its crew in the pens. *Far right U-Boat in a heavy storm*

The western approaches

A U-Boat slews round to evade a
Sunderland depth charge attack. This
U-Boat submerged, re-surfaced three
minutes later with severe damage, and
was promptly sunk

Where was Doenitz to turn next in his search for the answer to this terrible rout his forces were suffering? Wherever he sent them, they seemed to fall foul of the escorts, and always, when they returned to base, too many faces were conspicuous by their absence from among the crews which had sailed with such bravery and enthusiasm.

Doenitz chose, in fact, while maintaining a few boats on long range missions, to line up the majority for the onslaught of the coming year in the western approaches to the British Isles. He had stationed two dozen of them, by the middle of January, in a line stretching from the Faeroes in the north to Brest in the south. The boats patrolled some thirty miles apart, staying under water except when it became necessary to re-charge their batteries. In the circumstances the chances of sighting a convoy were no better than slim, but that task was now mainly in the hands of the Luftwaffe, whose signals of sightings would then be relayed to the U-Boats.

It was through no fault of the U-Boat arm that the plan never got off the ground. Several sightings were made, but in each case the outcome was the same. On January 17th, for example, the aircraft picked up a convoy and the U-Boats were ordered to attack, but the reconnaissance planes failed to keep in contact with the merchantmen, and only one U-Boat caught up before all track of the convoy's position was lost. That was U-641, which was promptly sunk by the corvette Violet. Doenitz ordered the patrols to move closer to the coast of Ireland, but his signals were intercepted by the British Admiralty and heavy concentrations of aircraft took up their station in Irish airfields. Their first task came on January 27th when the British heard Luftwaffe reconnaissance planes reporting the positions of two large convoys, and on the 28th of the month the U-Boats which went to search for them were themselves found by the defending aircraft. U-271 and U-571 were quickly sunk. Immediately the U-Boats called off this project, but the surface escorts continued to hunt them as they tried to escape to the west. On January 31st Captain Walker's Starling was among the boats which caught up and sank U-592.

During the following weeks, the air and sea defences kept a tight grip on these focal waters for Allied trans-oceanic shipping, and the U-Boats were never allowed to wrest the initiative from them. The U-Boat continued to make a number of attacks on

The attack goes on. The submarine's gun crew have been shot; it has no defence against the aircraft

The crew take to their one-man dinghies and await rescue as the boat goes down by the stern

reported convoys, but most of their time, fuel and energy, not to mention their morale, was sapped and wasted in trying to evade the destroyers, corvettes, and sloops of the Escort Groups. On February 8th *Woodpecker* accounted for U-762 with a barrage of depth charges. On the morning of the 9th, Walker in *Starling*, using his well tried 'creeping' technique in conjunction with another vessel, sank U-734. That same afternoon several destroyers joined in the macabre ritual on the surface above U-238, and she survived several attacks before succumbing. On February 11th the number of U-424 was added to the list of this group's victims.

The escort carrier *Fencer* had also been busy, and its aircraft sank U-666 on February 10th. That night aircraft flying from Ireland located and sank U-545 and U-283, this last boat being one of the few to achieve any success in this period: a few hours before she herself was sunk she had shot down one of the British aircraft.

Three days later, Doenitz, although he could at that time have no clear idea of the full extent of his losses, moved his boats further to the west, principally for their own safety. More convoys came into the area of their patrols, but the Luftwaffe's reconnaissance planes, suffering somewhat from inexperience compared with their British counterparts in the air, failed to report most of them. In the remote cases where contact was made, the story was always the same – either the aircraft forced the U-Boats to submerge, or the surface patrols came creeping along their paths with the mocking, menacing 'ping' of the asdic that made them forget about attacking merchant ships and turn their thoughts to their own safety.

On February 19th, it was Walker, almost inevitably, who destroyed the first U-Boat ever to put to sea fitted with the new schnorkel, U-264. Then at 10pm that night the U-Boats notched up their first and only success against the escorts of this whole period, when one of them struck home with an acoustic torpedo to the stern of the sloop *Woodpecker*, and she sank eight days later while under tow to the Scilly Isles.

For a nearly a month, the 2nd Escort Group had chased up and down the convoy routes seeking out U-Boats wherever they were indiscreet enough to show themselves, and the U-Boats had been powerless to do the slightest thing about it. Eleven of them were lost, and they had managed to sink only *Woodpecker*, a convoy straggler, and two aircraft.

When he learned of the U-Boats' lack of success, and the numbers he had lost, Doenitz was understandably bitter, and it was on the air reconnaissance planes that he heaped the blame. He took his complaints straight to Hitler, and on February 26th asked for more aircraft and a speed-up in

the building programme of the Type XXI boats, with their higher submerged speeds and Walter hulls, in which he placed so much faith.

In the meantime, he pushed his boats still further to the west, into the Atlantic, 700 miles from the shores of Europe, where they were ordered to operate individually against the convoys. They made several contacts, without any help from the aircraft, and U-575 succeeded, on March 8th, in sinking the corvette *Asphodel*. But that was one of the few encounters that went in their favour. U-575 herself learned the measure of the determination of the escorts at this stage of the battle. She was hunted for eighteen hours before escaping. U-358 had already suffered the longest continuous hunt of the whole war on February 29th, which lasted for thirty-eight hours, and on March 5th the crew of U-744 sweated out a hunt lasting thirty hours before they too were caught and forced to abandon ship.

By March 22nd even Doenitz had had enough, and he called the U-Boats out of the central Atlantic altogether, making it clear to Hitler that only the development of the new Type XXI boat and greatly increased help from the Luftwaffe would induce him to return there. He had lost, after all, thirty-six U-Boats between January and March. Another half dozen were added to this total during April, from the small numbers that still worked the fringes of the Atlantic, and of the five boats still there at the beginning of May, two were sunk during the month.

By the end of May, activities in distant theatres had also ground to a halt. Only two boats covered the waters off the American coast, and two the coast of West Africa. In nine months, these areas had produced together the sinking of only twenty-six Allied ships, at a cost of twelve U-Boats. Neither figure was enough to sway the course of the war either way. But to the Allies, saving ships meant success, for the process of building up supplies and arms in Europe could go on. To the Germans, on the other hand, the U-Boat war was an offensive war, and only the continual reduction in the numbers of ships able to sail the oceans of the world could be deemed progress. As long as the war was quiet, the Allies were winning it.

In June and July, a steady trickle of U-Boats left for operations in distant theatres, and the regular cycle of attack and counter-attack, of sinking and hunting, with torpedoes and depth charges, went on, but with none of the fury of the battle of previous years. The two sides, having got the measure of each other, preferred now to probe and spar, the Germans to seek out

A close eye on the depth and trim equipment as the boat submerges

soft spots in the defence and lunge, then withdraw, and the Allies to fly a constant vigil over their convoys, and strike as and when the enemy showed himself. During the months of June and July the U-Boats sank no ships off the American continent and none in the North Atlantic. It was a quiet time indeed.

The last few months had shown that neither the acoustic torpedo, nor a radar receiving device sensitive enough to give warning of the approach of aircraft using the ten centimetre equipment, nor the increased armament with which the U-Boats could keep the attackers at bay and sometimes even shoot their way out of trouble, had been enough to restore the balance in favour of the U-Boats. By June 1st Doenitz, having looked again at the future of the U-Boat arm, had settled his mind on what was to be his policy.

'Our efforts to tie down enemy forces have so far been successful,' he wrote in his war diary. 'The numbers of enemy aircraft and escort vessels, U-Boat killer groups and aircraft carriers allotted to anti-U-Boat forces, far from decreasing, has increased. For the submariners themselves the task of carrying on the fight solely for the purpose of tying down enemy forces is a particularly hard one.'

So that was it! After the years of aggressive, spirited sinking of merchant ships by the eager men of the U-Boat arm, after all Doenitz's bitter battles with his own superiors to allow him to wage his war against the enemy's supply lines as he thought it should be waged, after his magnificent convoy duels which had brought down shipping at the rate of three quarters of a million tons sunk per month, the U-Boat arm must now be resigned to the secondary task of tying down the enemy forces. They must act as bait to keep occupied the enemy's air and sea escort patrols, to draw his fire while other arms of the German nation, more important now, could carry on the task of fighting to win the war. And even that job could only be done in certain selected waters, where the U-Boats, with limited air cover and co-operation, could cope with the strength of the forces pitted against them. Worst of all, Doenitz noted, the chances of a crew not returning from an operation had greatly increased. Only 70 per cent of the men who went on patrol in the few months up to June 1944 had got back alive.

Yet, however defensive it was, however contrary it was to the fighting spirit of the U-Boat arm, tying down the enemy forces was a worthwhile task. As the ships carried war materials to the troops massing in Britain for the invasion of the continent, which everyone knew would ultimately be attempted, any aircraft or ship kept occupied was one aircraft or ship which the Allies could not throw into their offensive against the German forces in Europe. And if the U-Boats should happen to sink any ships, so much the better. The tanks, guns, vehicles, fuel, food, ammunition, and men to fight against the German troops would all, when the invasion came, have to be taken across the English Channel in ships, and any single vessel that the U-Boats could sink would hamper the invading armies and lighten the task of the defenders by just that significant amount.

There was, too, a glimmer of light on the distant horizon which promised a turn in the U-Boats' fortunes. In the spring of 1944 the schnorkel was being fitted in operational U-Boats in greater numbers, and in the month preceding the invasion enough experience of its capabilities and performance had been gained to confirm the early promise it had shown as a counter measure to the Allied anti-U-Boat techniques. Consequently, on June 1st, Doenitz issued orders that no U-Boats should be sent into the Atlantic unless equipped with the new device, and for the first time since 1940 the U-Boats were able to resume operations in the shallow waters of the English Channel.

When the invasion did come, on June 6th, they were able to prove their value. On that day Doenitz, well knowing the difficulties his men faced, made clear his attitude in an instruction to the first U-Boats to sail:

'Every vessel taking part in the landing, even if it has but a handful of men or but a solitary tank aboard, is a target of the utmost importance which must be attacked regardless of risk.'

'Every effort will be made to close the enemy invasion fleet regardless of danger from shallow water, possible minefields, or anything else.'

'Every man and weapon destroyed *before* reaching the beaches lessens the enemy's chances of ultimate success.'

'Every boat that inflicts losses on the enemy while he is landing has fulfilled its primary function even though it perishes in so doing.'

It was on that desperate, almost suicidal note, that the Admiral sent his men into the battle.

Above right Now that their torpedoes are spent, the crew can return to their bunks, no longer needed for storage. *Below right* After a heavy storm, repairs are needed to the radio aerial

The last defence

Soon after U-Boat command received the first reports of the invasion fleet setting sail, at about one o'clock in the morning of June 6th, the U-Boats were deployed to their anti-invasion stations. Twenty-one boats, five of them fitted with the schnorkel, were lying in Bergen in Norway. Nine schnorkel-fitted boats in Brest and La Pallice went to the English Channel between the Isle of Wight and Cherbourg. Seven boats from Brest without the schnorkel were ordered to seek out supply convoys between the Lizard and Start Point, on the British south coast. And nineteen other boats from the French bases were ordered to take up positions in a patrol line across the Bay of Biscay to oppose any Allied landings there.

That night, there began some of the fiercest and bitterest fighting of the whole U-Boat campaign, and the boats in the Bay of Biscay took some of the worst of it. They shot down four attacking aircraft, and although five U-Boats were forced back to port with damage, only U-955 was lost. The next night U-970 was sunk by a Sunderland, and U-629 and U-373 were destroyed by the same Liberator bomber within a short space of time. In those first few days, the value of the schnorkel, if only as a defensive measures, was amply and quickly demonstrated. When U-740 was sunk on June 9th and U-821 the next day, all sailings by boats not fitted with the schnorkel were can-celled, and those already at sea were recalled.

By June 15th the schnorkel boats from Norway were coming into the Channel. U-767 scored the first success by sinking a frigate near Land's End, and U-764 followed this by sinking another, though she was damaged in the counter attack. U-767 was also attacked three days later and sunk by three destroyers. After U-621 sank a land-ing ship close to the invasion area, the anti-invasion effort by the U-Boats came almost to a full stop. Those boats sailing from Norway were severely dealt with by British, Canadian and Norwegian air patrols, and between June 11th and 24th four U-Boats were sunk. In the last two weeks of June twelve more boats from the Biscay bases and the Atlantic began to converge on the Channel invasion area, but only three of them ever got there. U-948 was the only one which succeeded in inflic-ting any damage on supply shipping, when it torpedoed four ships one after another off Selsey Bill, three of which were lost, and one towed to port. Of the others, three were sunk by the escorts and the rest made such slow progress, sailing submerged on their schnorkels for most of the time, that they never reached the crowded cross channel routes where shipping was so plentiful.

During July, the U-Boats continued to sail in small numbers for the Channel, but their success was severely limited by

The deck crew take cover against the conning tower as a depth charge explodes

Type 'Biber'

One-man craft, of which 324 were put into service. It was hoped to transport these in hundreds by road to a point where with their limited range they could attack the invasion fleets.

$6\frac{1}{4}$ tons: $29\frac{1}{2} \times 5\frac{1}{4} \times 4\frac{3}{4}$ feet: 1-shaft petrol/electric motors, BHP/SHP $32/13 = 6\frac{1}{2}/5\frac{1}{4}$ knots (125/10 m at 6/5 k): two 21-inch torpedoes: complement 1

the strength and determination of the anti-submarine forces. U-390 torpedoed and sank a vessel on July 4th, but was herself sunk in the counter attack the next day. On July 6th U-678 went down, on July 8th U-234, and July 11th U-1222.

One boat which acquitted itself admirably during the invasion was U-763. On July 6th its captain, Ernst Cordes, counted 550 depth charges when he was located by destroyers during an attack off Selsey Bill. For thirty hours they chased him, and he darted about the shallow waters, changing direction as often as possible, and several times scraping the sea bed. By the morning of July 7th he had evaded all attacks and the destroyers had gone, but in the panic and exhaustion of the hunt, navigation by dead reckoning had been, to put it mildly, inaccurate. By mid-day on the 7th he estimated that the U-Boat should be about twenty miles north of Cherbourg, but all the indications failed to confirm that supposition. The depths were wrong according to the charts and the echo sounder, and the radio beacon produced the wrong fix. Cordes concluded that the currents had pushed them between the Channel Islands and he therefore steered north, still submerged, to try to extricate his boat from the mess and get into deeper water. But at four o'clock the next morning U-763 ran aground again. Having had time to consider the past hours, and add up the evidence, it slowly dawned on Cordes that he was miles from the Channel Islands. In fact, he realized, he had grounded in Spithead, the English anchorage off the Isle of Wight. These waters were alive with shipping of all kinds – landing craft, hospital ships from the invasion, boats working between the harbours along that busy coast. For twelve hours the U-Boat lay as still as a wreck on the sea-bed, then when the tide was right Cordes lifted her off and slowly crept out of those shallows. Eventually Cordes and his crew made their way back to Brest none the worse, except for the wear on their nerves, for that terrifying experience.

But most of the U-Boats that went into the Channel in that period were less lucky. By the beginning of August eight were added to the seven which had been sunk during June in the Bay of Biscay and English Channel. These were two-thirds of the boats which were sent on operations, and some 750 men perished in them. But still new recruits volunteered for service. No wonder Doenitz was prompted to remark of the anti-invasion campaign – 'In the end I myself could no longer match the moral fortitude displayed by the U-Boat crews.'

Their achievement was, in terms of numbers, disappointing – only twelve merchant ships, four landing craft, and five escorts were sunk, and five ships, one escort vessel, and one landing craft were

damaged. On the other hand, despite their losses, Doenitz considered their achievements useful. They had certainly not succeeded in stopping the invasion, but they had at least hampered the build-up of Allied troops, and that, he thought, had lightened the load of the defending troops ashore.

Most important, the use of the schnorkel in this campaign had shown that the pendulum, at last, might be starting to swing the other way. After the supremacy of the U-Boat against the convoy routes during the first years of the war, followed by their defeat in 1943 by the air and sea escorts, the answer was now plainly in sight. With the schnorkel the U-Boats had proved almost immune from airborne radar, which at this stage of its development appeared to be incapable of picking up an echo from such a small object as a schnorkel head. At that time, their slow underwater speed and their limited vision from the periscope combined to reduce the effectiveness of the U-Boat. But the building programme for the high speed versions was now under way, and when they came forward in great numbers the prospect of mounting a new campaign with lightning strikes under water looked excellent. It would be a new kind of warfare. But then, after nearly five years of hostilities, a new kind of warfare was exactly what was required.

The value of the schnorkel was best demonstrated in the first week in August, when the breakthrough of American forces opened their way to the Brittany peninsular and threatened to cut off the U-Boat bases at Brest and Lorient. Faced with this threat, Doenitz ordered his boats south to the bases at La Pallice and Bordeaux. Then in mid-August, the American forces reached the outskirts of the Biscay bases and all the U-Boats were ordered to sail to Norway. Despite the Allied awareness of this move and their determined air effort to cut it off, twenty-two boats were successfully transferred, together with nine others which were either operating in the Channel or coming into base after long range sorties. It was almost wholly due to the schnorkel that they were able to evade destruction during the passage through crowded waters.

But there were disadvantages. While a boat was using its schnorkel and recharging its batteries submerged, the sea was liable to slop over the top, closing the float valve which prevented water pouring into the boat. When that happened, the diesel engines were bound to take oxygen from the only other available source, the interior of the hull, which not only left the men gasping with an oxygen shortage, but subjected them to severe and sudden changes of pressure. At the same time, the exhaust gases were blown back into the boat and the high carbon dioxide content

German crew abandon their sinking U-Boat. 12 men survived

in the burnt diesel fumes added to the men's problems. The schnorkel itself, moreover, left a trail of foam behind it as well as a cloud of exhaust gases, as the U-Boat went forward at half speed on batteries while the diesel engines were running to charge them up. Consequently, it soon became possible to use the instrument only at night, while the men by day lay in their bunks to conserve oxygen, not moving about the boat, not cooking or eating or talking, coming alive only at night when it was safe to raise the schnorkel. Then, with cold air blowing through the boat, even if it meant continual changes in pressure as the water closed off the valves, the crews attacked their physical jerks like athletes to restore air to their lungs and circulation to their unused limbs. After such long hours and days without the sight of daylight, fatigue among the U-Boat crews grew alarmingly, and the time a U-Boat could spend at sea was reduced to about half the average of the early years of the war.

The advent of the schnorkel also induced the anti-U-Boat forces to expend considerable effort, fuel, and high explosive on 'phantom' sightings. As their real sightings became fewer and fewer, their imaginations grew more and more lively. While the U-Boats made their voyages unharmed, air escort pilots and observers spent their time chasing and attacking the whisps of foam and small water spouts – 'willywaws' to the sailor – that the seas constantly threw up. Even innocent spouting whales were often subjected to the indignity of a severe depth charging.

As the U-Boats from Biscay made their way to Norway and northern Germany, and then set out again for operations in British coastal waters, they used their schnorkels to good effect. After the collapse of the Biscay bases, patrols by British aircraft had been heavily reinforced over the passage between Shetland and Iceland, but of the sixteen boats which passed through those waters by the end of August, only two were ever sighted from the air, and even those were not attacked.

On the other hand, in view of the need of the U-Boats to use that northern passage, the British had replied by routing convoys to the south of Ireland, with the result that little contact was made, and the campaign dragged on towards the end of the year with all the characteristics of a tedious stalemate. In each of the months of September, October, and November only one U-Boat was sunk in the northern transit routes, and in December fifty U-Boats made the passage without a single casualty. But sinkings were rare. Even after they had successfully negotiated the passage, their slow underwater speed and limited peris-

cape vision deprived the U-Boats of much of their power. There were two notable exceptions. U-482, under Count von Matushka, between August 16th and September 26th travelled over 2,700 miles, mostly under water, and sank four ships from two convoys plus an escorting corvette. Then in December U-486 sank three merchant ships, a troopship carrying 800 soldiers, and a frigate, all in the English Channel. But these individual achievements were not enough to alter the colourless complexion of the general picture.

In the last four months of 1944 the battle that smouldered on in British coastal waters, and burned even more slowly elsewhere in the world, resulting in the sinking of only twenty-four ships, while fifty-five U-Boats were destroyed. It seemed that the whole campaign had ground down with ignominy to the proportions of a mock battle. But Doenitz knew, greatly to his satisfaction, and the British Admiralty knew, greatly to their trepidation, that the building programme for the U-Boat was going ahead at an increasing rate, and that it was based on the new high underwater speed Type XXI and XXIII boats, against which no Allied answer appeared immediately available.

Unless the British succeeded quickly in pushing up the numbers of U-Boats sunk, and forced an early decision on the issue, before the U-Boat arm built up its strength and snatched the initiative from them, there was still the possibility of a German return to supremacy. As the year turned the stage was set for what promised to be one of the most intriguing and unpredictable phases in the war.

Type XXIC

An advanced design of 'U' Boat using to full extent the 'schnorkel' breathing service which enabled the craft to use their diesel engines while running submerged.

Note the torpedo tubes mounted just in front of the conning tower. These twelve tubes (six either side) fired the torpedoes astern ten degrees off from the centre line. Six tubes were also mounted in the bow

The invention that transformed the U-Boats; Professor Walter's schnorkel.

Displacement
1,621/1, 819 tons
Dimensions
$251\frac{3}{4} \times 21\frac{3}{4} \times 20\frac{1}{4}$ feet
Machinery
2-shaft diesel/electric motors, BHP/SHP
$4,000/5,000 = 15\frac{1}{2}/16$ knots; and silent
creeping electric motors, SHP
$226 = 5$ knots

Bunkers and radius
OF 250 tons; 11,150/285 miles at 12/6 knots
Armament
Four 30 mm AA (2 × 2) guns; 18 21-inch
torpedo tubes
Complement
57

In action at sea

148

Boarding party on a captured U-Boat; US sailors prepare to tow U-505 to Bermuda, 2,500 miles away

The final phase: January to May 1945

In January 1945 the first of the Type XXIII boats, U-2324, left its Norwegian base and sailed round the north of the Shetland Isles to play its part, together with nineteen other boats, in the coastal campaign. These brought the total force in those waters to thirty-nine. It was a source of great pleasure to Doenitz to know that the schnorkel was rendering his boats totally immune from air attack during their passage to and from operational waters. In the whole of January not a single boat was lost on the transit routes. Communications with U-Boat headquarters was virtually impossible, of course, since the U-Boats sailed submerged almost the whole time, but on the other hand it effectively deprived the British submarine tracking room of its principal source of intelligence. Now it was only when the U-Boats made an attack that the escorts could even begin a search.

U-1055 was one of the first to achieve a success during this year, when on January 9th she sank a ship in the Irish Sea, and followed this up by sinking two more within the next two days. On January 15th U-482 carried out a torpedo attack off the east coast of Scotland, in which she sank one merchant ship and damaged the escort carrier *Thane*. But the escorts picked up contact with her, and after a hunt lasting several hours she was sunk. U-1172 was also sunk after a five hour hunt, as the result of

an attack in which she damaged a frigate. U-1051 was destroyed, on January 27th, and U-825 damaged, after they had attacked a convoy off the Isle of Man, and when U-1199, U-650, and U-1020 were sunk, the month closed on more or less level terms, with six U-Boats destroyed and seven Allied ships sunk. But by the end of January Doenitz was even more firmly convinced that his schnorkel had opened up new possibilities, even if only older designed boats were equipped with it before the new types came forward. He decided to intensify the campaign in the British coastal waters by sending there all the new boats commissioned during February. Apart from their immunity from air attack, they were also, in those shallow waters with strong tides and tortuous currents, well protected from detection by the asdic. It looked as if this new operation would at last allow the U-Boats to revert to the twin functions which they had developed; they would in all probability be able once more to begin sinking enemy ships on a greater scale, which would contribute enormously to the task of the armies in Europe, and they would also continue to tie down enemy escorts in their own home waters, so that no surface vessels could be released to mount an offensive campaign against the stream of German ships carrying supplies and reinforcements for these troops.

In February, forty-one U-Boats sailed

from the northern bases with high hopes, particularly for the English Channel. Unhappily, their achievements failed to meet expectations. They managed to sink only seven ships, including two escorts, in the Channel, and three in the Irish Sea. Other sinkings out in the western approaches during February raised the number of successes to eleven merchantmen and three escort vessels, but the cost to the U-Boat arm was no less than twelve.

March produced even worse results. Thirty-seven U-Boats sailed from the Norway bases to join in the fighting, bringing the total at the end of the month to fifty-three in coastal waters. But the surface and air escorts, together with deep minefields which the British had resorted to, accounted for fifteen U-Boats, while they in their turn could only claim the destruction of ten merchant ships and three escorts. Once more, it transpired, the U-Boat arm had based their anticipation for a new phase of battle on a static estimation of the enemy's capability. In fact, of course, developments were still continually being introduced, and several devices unpredicted by the Germans contributed to their increasing losses.

The 'squid' was coming into use as a useful complementary weapon to the well-proven 'hedgehog'. This, instead of firing a carpet of twenty-four contact charges, fired three, to explode in close proximity to the U-Boat's hull. If the 'squid' failed to sink the U-Boat outright, damage caused by concussion would force it to the surface, where it was instantly despatched.

A new and sensitive radar set, working on the three centimetre wavelength and capable of picking up an echo from the schnorkel, was added to the armoury, though in certain instances, particularly in inshore waters, this led to a large number of mistaken sightings by confusing a schnorkel echo with that from odd bits of floating debris.

Once a positive sighting was obtained, the aircraft had a formidable new weapon in their 600lb bomb, in addition to the 300lb depth charge. With the aid of a new low altitude bomb sight, these explosives were used with devastating accuracy to the cost of a number of U-Boats.

But the most novel weapon in the escort's book was a new 'sono' buoy invented by the Americans, which could be planted in a likely U-Boat area and would automatically pick up and transmit to an aircraft noises from a U-Boat's propellor. A small acoustic torpedo dropped in the region of the U-Boat would then home on to its target. The war was becoming increasingly automated.

In April the battle remained constant, and the U-Boats, for the loss of fifteen of their number, sank ten merchant vessels and three warships. But sad as the losses

were to the U-Boat arm, they were offset by the encouraging rate at which the new boats were now coming into service. In April forty-four, including the first Type XXI boat, left the Norwegian bases, and as long as the rate at which they were commissioned outran the rate at which they were sunk, the total U-Boat force, by virtue not only of its increasing numbers, but also of its growing proportion of new types, was becoming stronger and stronger. Apart from their high striking speeds under water, they could cruise at 5·5 knots for long periods in virtual silence, and their radius was sufficient for them to reach as far as the South Atlantic and operate there for a month before returning home. With a host of newly designed and sophisticated instruments, they could also operate 'blind', firing their torpedoes from a depth of 150 feet. It is significant that while the U-Boat arm was losing so many of its vessels, almost all those destroyed were the early designs with slow under-water speeds.

The building programme of new U-Boats, which had been severely disrupted in the previous November when Allied bombing raids blocked the Dortmund, Ems, and Mittelland canals was, by May, restored to such an extent that twelve Type XXI boats were ready to join the one already in service, and another ninety-one were at sea for crew training or trials. But by then the end was in sight. Events on land had finally imposed irrevocable defeat on the German army.

At 3.14pm on May 4th Doenitz broadcast to all his U-Boat commanders instructions to cease fire. For the Allies, their success in the land battles had come just in time, for many more months might have led to overwhelmingly superiority of the newly equipped U-Boat arm. How effective the new boats were was shown by Lt-Cdr Schnee, in one of the Type XXIs, U-2511. Schnee had already, before the surrender, discovered the degree of immunity which the underwater power of the huge electric battery lent. In the North Sea he had encountered an anti-submarine group, but with a simple deflection of his course through 30 degrees, he was able with consummate ease to escape submerged, and in a short time lose the 'ping' of the asdic. The Type XXI U-Boat could, after all, make as good underwater speed as many of the escort vessels could make on the surface. Then, shortly after receiving the ceasefire order – Schnee was one of only eight commanders who obeyed at once – he encountered a British cruiser and several destroyers while on the way from the North Sea to Bergen He delivered a dummy run under water, and came within 500 yards of the cruiser. Later events showed that the British had no idea how near to destruction their cruiser had been. Schnee

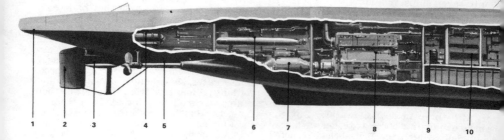

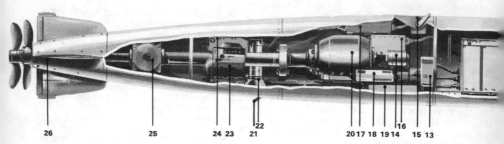

Type VII U-Boat

1 Aft torpedo exit

2 Rudder, port and starboard

3 Hydroplane, port and starboard

4 Aft torpedo tubes and engineer ratings' quarters

5 Propellor shaft, port and starboard

6 Spare torpedo

7 Electric motors, port and starboard, for underwater propulsion, and engine room quarters

8 Main diesel engine, port and starboard

9 Escape hatch

10 Officers' mess

11 Batteries

12 Main control room

13 Twin wells for lowered search and attack periscopes

14 Midships ballast/trim tank

15 Commander's cabin

16 Batteries

17 Crew's mess

18 Galley

19 Six torpedoes in racks, Some of the crew have to sleep on or in between these torpedoes

20 Forward torpedo tubes, two port, two starboard

21 Forward torpedo doors

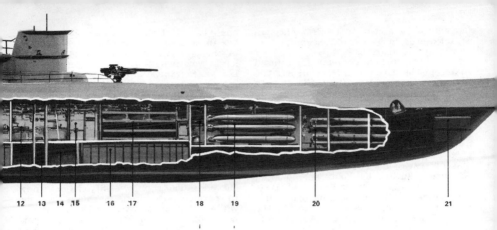

12 13 14 15 16 17 18 19 20 21

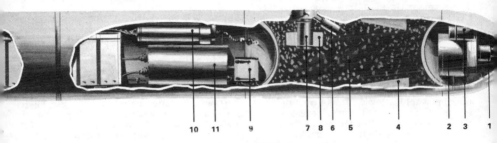

10 11 9 7 8 6 5 4 2 3 1

Type V German acoustic torpedo

1 Acoustic receiver
2 Acoustic amplifier
3 Thermal relay for safety range
4 Pick up coils
5 Warhead
6 Oolenoid locking pistol propellor
7 Contact (inertia) pistol
8 Coil operating pistol
9 Fusing relay
10 Pistol amplifier
11 Compressed air reservoir
12 36-cell battery
13 Main switch (motor circuit)

14 Charging plug
15 Starting lever
16 Electric generator for homing gear supply
17 G Switch
18 Resistance converter for pistol supply
19 Pistol distributor box
20 Motor
21 Touching lever switch
22 Depth control gear
23 Gyroscope
24 Discriminator box
25 Contra rotating gear
26 Tail unit and propellors

judged the new boat to be first class in attack and defence – 'something completely new to any submariner.'

Many of the U-Boat commanders refused to accept the ceasefire order, still less the broadcast instructions from the British Admiralty on May 8th for them all to surface, report their positions, and steam immediately to specified ports. The first surrenders began to take place on May 9th, and others followed during the next few days. Some U-Boats made for German ports still submerged, and others made for distant parts, two of them reaching Argentina. In all, 156 boats surrendered, but the greater proportion of U-Boat commanders regarded handing over their boats to the enemy as a violation of the code of honour of fighting men. Doenitz himself refused to give the order for the U-Boats to be scuttled. Hitler had by then made his disappearance, and under the terms of his will Doenitz had taken over as head of state. His aim was to secure a speedy and orderly end to the war, and save as many German lives as possible. The British had stipulated that the surrender should not be accompanied by the destruction of weapons and the sinking of warships, and to maintain British trust Doenitz refused to issue the code word for wholesale scuttling – *Regenbogen* (rainbow). It was on the personal initiative of the U-Boat commanders, incredulous that their commander would allow the fleet to fall into enemy hands unless under pressure or threat, that the whisper went by radio through the U-Boats in the German ports – '*Regenbogen*'. The crews put to sea in large numbers and soon the explosions were echoing round the waters of the North Sea and the Baltic. In all 221 boats were scuttled.

It was the end of a tenacious but unsuccessful attempt by Germany to bring the Allies to their knees by severing their main artery, the ocean shipping routes on which their life depended. At times Germany came close to achieving this aim. In the great Atlantic battles of the early years, when a monthly loss of up to three quarters of a million tons of shipping was as much as the Allies could replace, and vital cargoes of oil, arms and machinery were sent to rot on the sea bed, it seemed that the course of the war was moving steadily in Germany's favour.

Then the escorts' growing skill, increasing numbers, and technical superiority, together with the failure of the Germans to place sufficient faith in, or divert sufficient resources to, their U-Boat building programme, swung the balance in favour of the Allies.

Finally the pendulum started to swing once more, as the new U-Boats started to come into commission, and not even the most energetic operations by air and sea could banish them from the very shores of the British Isles. But in the early months of the new era the quantity of shipping sunk was insignificant – never, in the last year of war, more than 100,000 tons per month, and on average little more than half that total. What might have happened had the end of the war been delayed by six months or a year, until the new boats came into their own, and until ultimately the advanced Walter hydrogen peroxide boat came into commission, is a problem of the most inscrutable kind. Certainly the prospect had the Allies worried. Churchill himself has written of the U-Boat threat at the end: 'The schnorkel-fitted boats now in service, breathing through a tube while charging their batteries submerged, were but an introduction to the new pattern of U-Boat warfare which Doenitz had planned. He was counting on the advent of the new type of boat, of which very many were now being built. The first of these were already under trial. Real success for Germany depended on their early arrival in service in large numbers. Their high submerged speed threatened us with new problems, and would indeed, as Doenitz predicted, have revolutionised U-Boat warfare.'

Before this revolution could come to full fruition, German U-Boats sank no less than 2,603 merchant ships – a total of over 13½ million tons – and in addition they claimed 175 Allied naval vessels. But their own losses were considerable. The Germans built 1,162 U-Boats, and of this total 784 were lost through various causes.

In human terms, the cost to both sides was stupendous. More than 40,900 men were recruited into the U-Boat arm in the course of the war, of whom a total of 28,000 lost their lives, and another 5,000 were taken prisoner. The Allies suffered even bitterer carnage – more than 30,000 men killed from the British Merchant Navy alone, together with many more thousands of merchant seamen from other countries. Of the Royal Navy's full wartime list of over 70,000 men and women, a large proportion gave their lives in the fight against the U-Boats.

In the final analysis, it is perhaps fitting that the result of Germany's struggle for mastery of the sea-lanes should be measured in terms of the destruction of human life.

Mass production of U-Boats; at the end of the war 17 were being built at Bremen in sections for assembly on the launching way

The final product ; the sections are being
joined together in the Bremen yard and
a new generation of submarines is almost
ready for launching

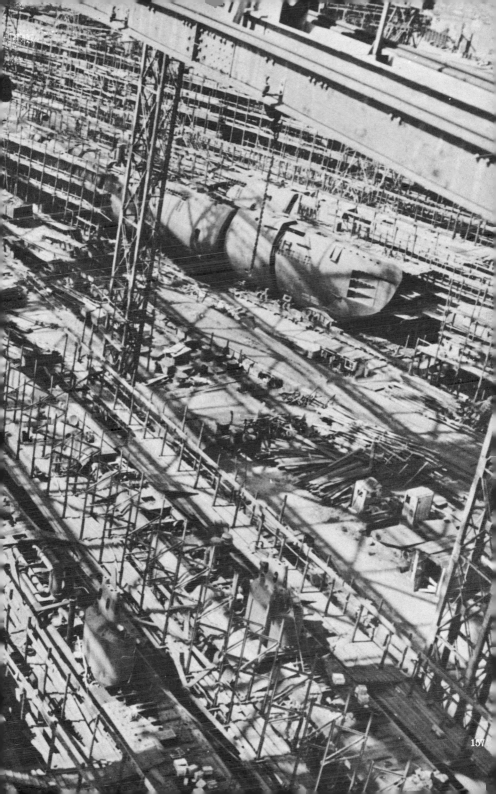

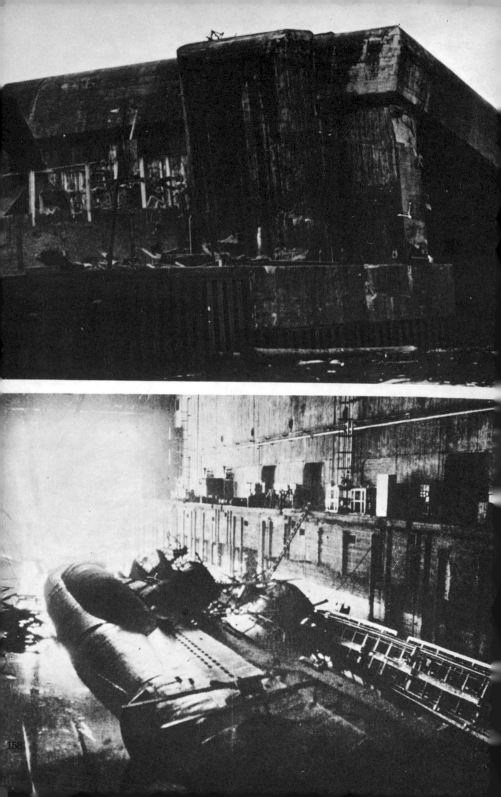

As well as scuttling many of their boats the Germans destroyed their own U-Boat pens at Hamburg with 32 tons of Luftwaffe bombs. *Below left* An RAF success; a 12,000 lb bomb has penetrated the roof of a pen and destroyed two boats. *Below right* At the end of the war, some U-Boats survived undamaged in the pens at Trondhiem

Bibliography

The Submarine and Sea Power Sir Arthur Hezlet (Peter Davies, London. Stein and Day, New York)
Memoirs Admiral Dönitz (Weidenfeld and Nicolson, London. World, New York)
H M Submarine P K Kemp (Herbert Jenkins, London)
British Navies in the Second World War Sir W M James (Longmans, London)
German Submarines Vols. 1 and 2 (MacDonald, London)
The Navy at War 1939–45 Captain S W Roskill (Collins, London)
The War at Sea Vols. 1 to 3 Captain S W Roskill (HMSO, London)
U-Boats at War Harold Busch (Ballantine Books, New York)
U-Boats 977 Heinz Schaeffer (Ballantine Books, New York)
The Sea Wolves Wolfgang Frank (Ballantine Books, New York)
Sharks and Little Fish Wolfgang Ott (Ballantine Books, New York)